# CALL to FAITH

## GRADE 4
*School*

**OurSundayVisitor**

Curriculum Division

www.osvcurriculum.com

The Subcommittee on the Catechism, United States Conference of Catholic Bishops, has found this catechetical series, © 2009 Edition, to be in conformity with the *Catechism of the Catholic Church.*

**Nihil Obstat**
Rev. Richard L. Schaefer

**Imprimatur**
✠ Most Rev. Thomas Wenski
Bishop of Orlando
December 14, 2007

The Imprimatur is an official declaration that a book or pamphlet is free of doctrinal or moral error. No implication is contained therein that anyone who granted the Imprimatur agrees with the contents, opinions, or statements expressed.

For permission to reprint copyrighted materials, grateful acknowledgment is made to the following sources:

*Confraternity of Christian Doctrine, Washington, D.C.:* Scriptures from the *New American Bible.* Text copyright © 1991, 1986, 1970 by the Confraternity of Christian Doctrine. All rights reserved. No part of the *New American Bible* may be used or reproduced in any form, without permission in writing from the copyright owner.

*Hinshaw Music, Inc.:* Lyrics from "Go Now in Peace" by Natalie Sleeth. Lyrics © 1976 by Hinshaw Music, Inc.

*Hope Publishing Co., Carol Stream, IL 60188:* Lyrics from "Jesu, Jesu" by Tom Colvin. Lyrics © 1969 by Hope Publishing Co. Lyrics from "Shout for Joy" by David Mowbray. Lyrics © 1982 by Jubilate Hymns, Ltd.

*Hyperion:* From "Peace of Patience" in *Journey Through Heartsongs* by Mattie Stepanek. Text copyright © 2001 by Mattie Stepanek.

The English translation of the "Come, Holy Spirit" (Retitled: "Prayer to the Holy Spirit"), Litany of Saint Joseph, *Angelus* and *Memorare* from *A Book of Prayers* © 1982, International Commission on English in the Liturgy Corporation (ICEL); excerpts from the English translation of *The Roman Missal* © 2010, ICEL; the English translation of "Psalm 117: Go Out to All the World" from *Lectionary for Mass* © 1969, 1981, 1997, ICEL; the English translation of the Act of Contrition from *Rite of Penance* © 1974, ICEL.

Additional acknowledgments appear on page 326.

Call to Faith School Grade 4 Student Book
ISBN: 978-0-15-902285-6
Item Number: CU1381

6 7 8 9 10 11 21 13 015016 19 18 17 16 15
Webcrafters, Inc., Madison, WI, USA; February 2015; Job# 120563

# Grade 4 Contents

# Catholic Source Book

# About You

## Let Us Pray

**Leader:** Loving God, help us to learn your way.
"Blessed are you, O LORD;
  teach me your laws."

*Psalm 119:12*

**All:** Loving God, help us to learn your way.

## Activity Let's Begin

**Looking Ahead** Welcome to the fourth grade. You have a whole new year of experiences ahead of you. You will have a new teacher, new classes, and possibly even new friends. You will learn more about your faith and about your life as a child of God.

You are special. What is the best thing about being you?

## What are some of your Favorite Things?

**Time of Day**
3AM, A.m

**Holiday**
Christmas

**Book**
Diary of a Minecraft zombie

# About Your Faith

You are about to begin the next mile of your faith journey, but you do not travel alone. Your family, friends, and the whole parish community travel with you. This year you will read Bible stories and learn more about being a part of the Catholic Church.

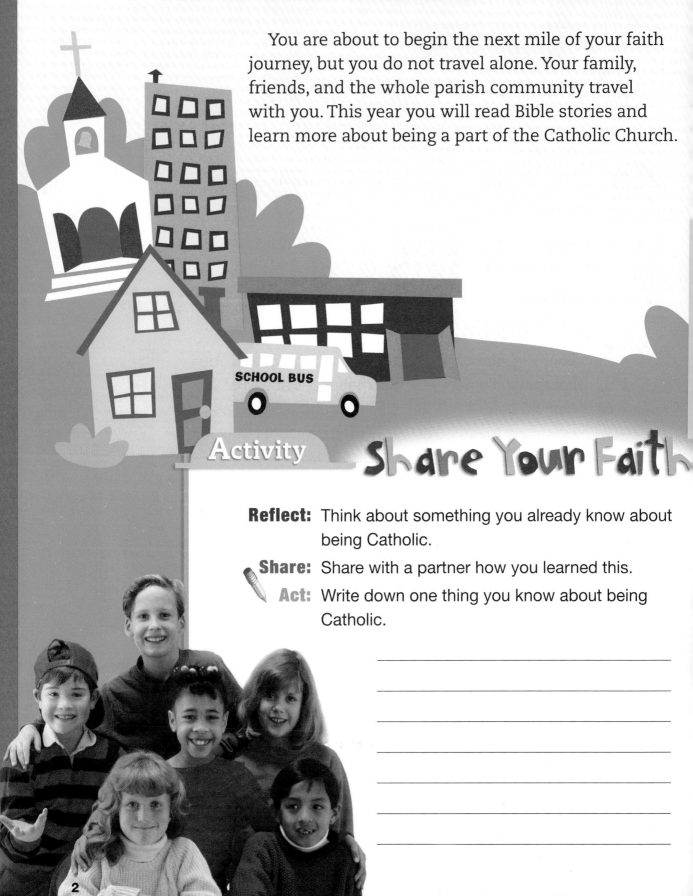

## Activity

### Share Your Faith

**Reflect:** Think about something you already know about being Catholic.

**Share:** Share with a partner how you learned this.

**Act:** Write down one thing you know about being Catholic.

_____

_____

_____

_____

_____

_____

2

# About Your Book

Your book will help you to learn more about your faith, important people of faith, and ways Catholics celebrate faith.

**Activity**     Connect Your Faith

**Go On A Scavenger Hunt** As you read your book, you will find lots of different things. To get to know your book, look for the features listed below. Write down where you find each of them.

✝ SCRIPTURE                    Page _____

BIOGRAPHY                      Page _____

Words of Faith                 Page _____

Faith Fact                     Page _____

People of Faith                Page _____

Let Us Pray                    Page _____

Focus                          Page _____

# A Call to Faith

## Gather

*Pray the Sign of the Cross together.*

Leader: Blessed be God.

All: **Blessed be God forever.**

Leader: Let us pray.
*Bow your heads as the leader prays.*

All: **Amen.**

## Listen to God's Word

Reader: A reading from the holy Gospel according to Matthew.
*Read Matthew 9:9–13.*
The Gospel of the Lord.

All: **Praise to you, Lord Jesus Christ.**

## Dialogue

Why do you think Jesus went and ate with Matthew after he called him to be a disciple?

How can you answer Jesus' call to follow him?

## Prayer of the Faithful

Leader: Lord, the first disciples answered your call. They believed in you and followed you. We believe in you, too. Please hear our prayers.
*Respond to each prayer with these words.*

All: **Lord, hear our prayer.**

## Answer the Call

Leader: Matthew responded to Jesus' call to follow him. He welcomed Jesus into his life and his home. You can welcome Jesus into your life, too.

*Come forward as your name is called. Bow to the cross and say aloud "I will follow you, Jesus."*

You are all followers of Jesus. Welcome one another with a sign of his peace.

# Go Forth!

Leader: Let us go forth to welcome Christ into our lives.

All: **Thanks be to God.**

*Sing together.*

We are called to act with justice,
we are called to love tenderly,
we are called to serve one another;
to walk humbly with God!

"We Are Called" © 1988, 2004, GIA Publications, Inc.

# The Church's Seasons

**D**ifferent things happen at different times during the year. During fall, school starts and the leaves change color. In winter trees are bare and the days are short. When spring comes the flowers bloom, the days get longer, and people want to spend time outside. Summer brings warmer days, school break, and long hours of fun.

The Church has seasons, too. The seasons of the Church year recall important events in the lives of Jesus, Mary, and the saints. In every season the Church prays together to remember all the gifts that come from God the Father and his Son, Jesus.

The Church prays using different words and actions. Here are some of them.

## Words and Actions

The Bible is honored by bowing and sitting before it in silence.

The Cross is honored by kneeling in front of it or kissing it.

The sign of Christ's peace is offered with a handshake.

The Sign of the Cross is marked on foreheads, hearts, and lips.

Holy water is used as a reminder of Baptism.

Your class will use these words and actions to celebrate the different seasons.

# The Church Year

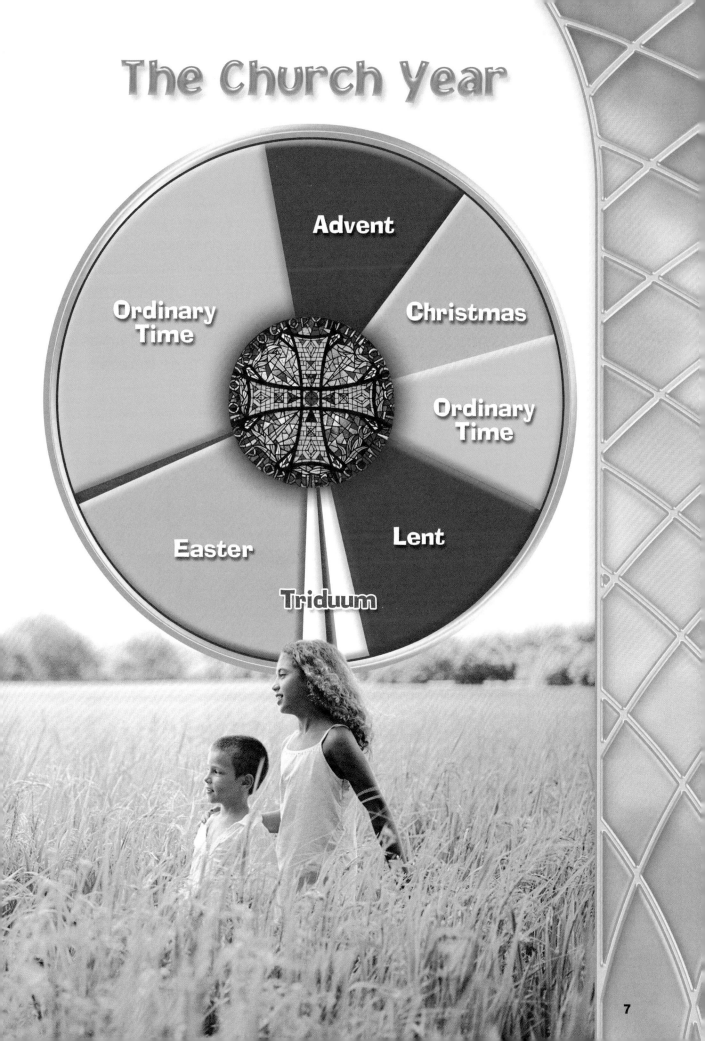

Advent

Christmas

Ordinary
Time

Ordinary
Time

Easter

Lent

Triduum

# Sorrowful Mother

The Church honors Mary in every season of the year. The feast days of Mary often remember happy events in Mary's life, such as the day of her birth or her Assumption into heaven. But on September 15 during Ordinary Time, the Church honors Mary as Our Lady of Sorrows. This feast is a time to recall some of the sorrows in Mary's life.

## Mary, Our Model of Faith

There were sad times in Mary's life. Her son was born far from her home, in Bethlehem. Mary and Joseph had to travel quickly to another country to protect the child Jesus from King Herod. Herod feared that Jesus was the long-awaited Messiah and wanted to kill him. Mary watched as many rejected her Son's message of love. And she stood sorrowfully at the foot of the cross as he died.

In difficult and sad times, Mary always believed in her Son. She acted with courage and cared for others. Mary can be a model for you, too, in the sad times of your life.

❓ **Who are some other role models in your life?**

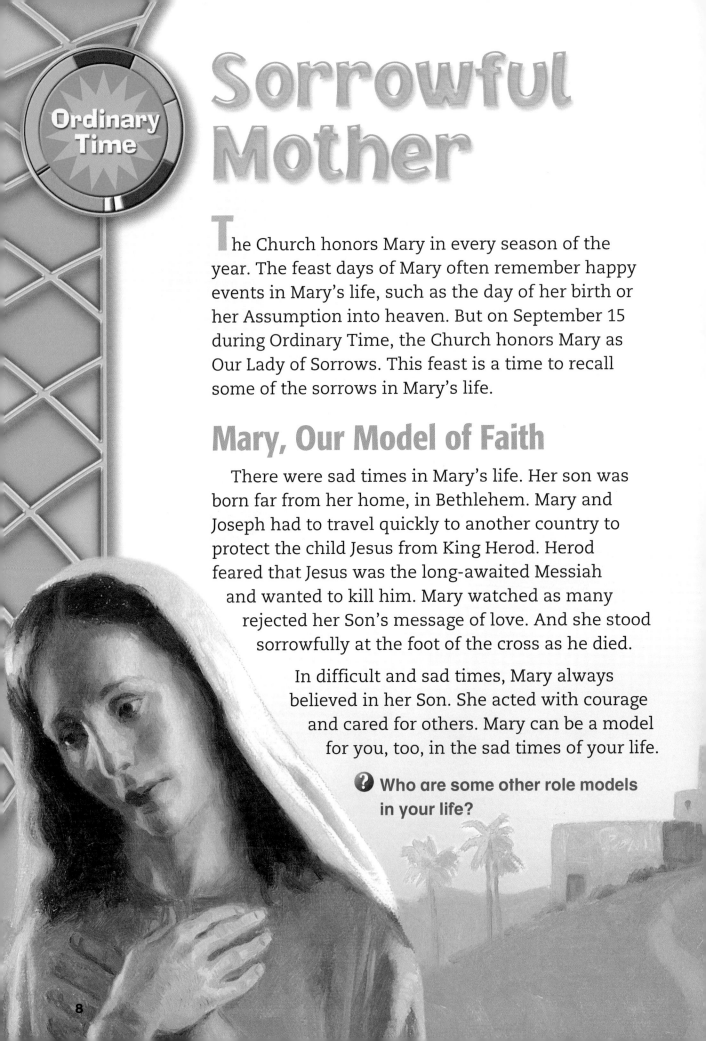

# Celebrate Mary

## Gather

*Pray the Sign of the Cross together.*

**Leader:** Blessed be God.

**All:** **Blessed be God forever.**

*Sing together.*

Take, O take me as I am;
summon out what I shall be;
Set your seal upon my heart
   and live in me.

"Take, O Take Me As I Am" © 1994, Iona Community,
GIA Publications, Inc., agent

**Leader:** Let us pray together for God's mercy.

Lord Jesus, you forgive us and rescue us from
the pain of sin.
Lord, have mercy.

**All:** **Lord, have mercy.**

**Leader:** Christ Jesus, you have given us Mary as
a model of courage and patience.
Christ, have mercy.

**All:** **Christ, have mercy.**

**Leader:** Lord Jesus, as we remember Mary's sorrows,
we express sorrow for our failure to love.
Lord, have mercy.

**All:** **Lord, have mercy.**

**Leader:** Let us pray.

*Bow your heads as the leader prays.*

**All:** **Amen.**

# Listen to God's Word

Reader: A reading from the holy Gospel according to Luke.

*Read Luke 2:22–35.*
The Gospel of the Lord.

All: **Praise to you, Lord Jesus Christ.**

## Dialogue

Why did Simeon's message cause Mary sorrow?

If you had been in the Temple, what question would you have asked Simeon?

## Meditation

*Sit in silence before the cross as the leader leads you in a meditation on Our Lady of Sorrows.*

Leader: Let us pray . . .

All: **Amen.**

# Go Forth!

Leader: Let us go forth in Mary's spirit of faith, hope, and love for her Son.

All: **Thanks be to God.**

*Sing together.*

Take, O take me as I am;
summon out what I shall be;
set your seal upon my heart
   and live in me.

"Take, O Take Me As I Am" © 1994, Iona Community, GIA Publications, Inc.

# Compassion

Mary watched as her Son suffered and died at the hands of those who did not understand him. Sorrow is still felt today whenever someone sees a loved one hurting. But from your sorrow can grow greater caring and compassion for the suffering of the whole world. Compassion for others is more powerful than pain. That is the message of the gospel.

**❓ When have you felt sorrow when someone you loved was hurting?**

**(ACTIVITY)**

## The Sorrowful Mysteries

The Sorrowful Mysteries name five events in Jesus' Passion. Each mystery can also teach you a virtue that will make you a stronger Christian. On separate paper, make a drawing of one of the Sorrowful Mysteries, or show a way that you can learn and live its virtue. Pray a decade of the Rosary on Tuesday or Friday of this week and reflect on the mystery you chose:

- The Agony in the Garden (repentance)
- The Scourging at the Pillar (purity)
- The Crowning with Thorns (courage)
- Carrying the Cross (patience)
- The Crucifixion (self-denial)

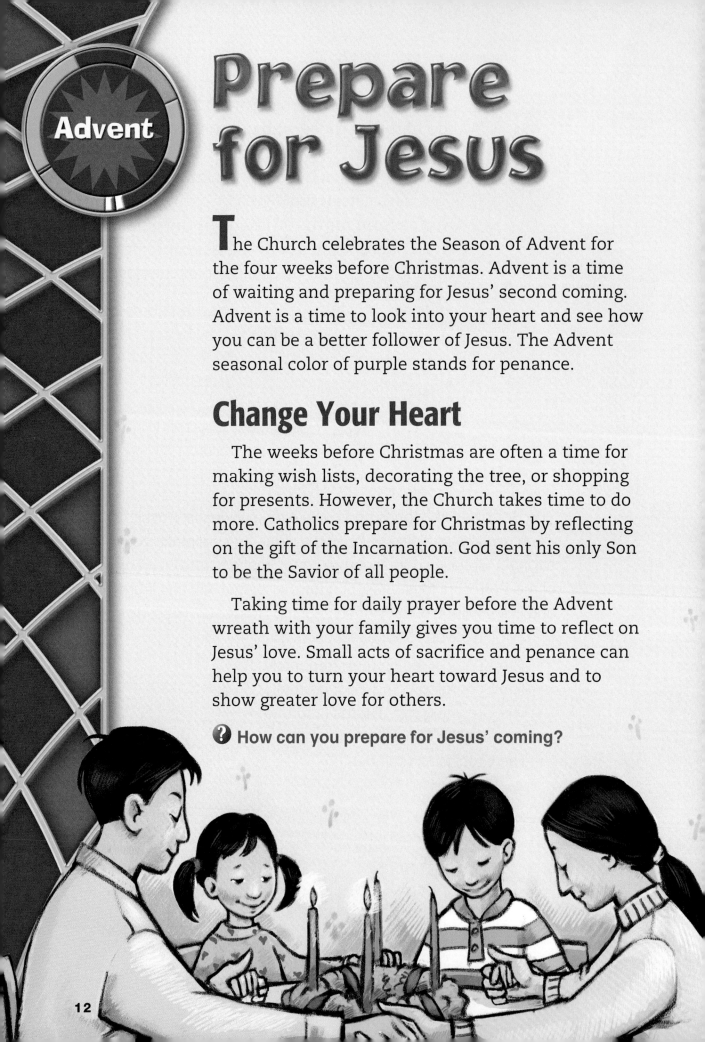

# Prepare for Jesus

The Church celebrates the Season of Advent for the four weeks before Christmas. Advent is a time of waiting and preparing for Jesus' second coming. Advent is a time to look into your heart and see how you can be a better follower of Jesus. The Advent seasonal color of purple stands for penance.

## Change Your Heart

The weeks before Christmas are often a time for making wish lists, decorating the tree, or shopping for presents. However, the Church takes time to do more. Catholics prepare for Christmas by reflecting on the gift of the Incarnation. God sent his only Son to be the Savior of all people.

Taking time for daily prayer before the Advent wreath with your family gives you time to reflect on Jesus' love. Small acts of sacrifice and penance can help you to turn your heart toward Jesus and to show greater love for others.

**?** **How can you prepare for Jesus' coming?**

# Celebrate Advent

## Gather

*Sing together the refrain.*

Come, O Lord, change our hearts!
Emmanuel, God is with us.

"Come, O Lord" © 1997, GIA Publications, Inc.

*Pray the Sign of the Cross together.*

**Leader:** Our help is in the name of the Lord.

**All:** **Who made heaven and earth.**

**Leader:** Let us pray.

*Bow your heads as the leader prays.*

**All:** **Amen.**

I confess to almighty God
and to you, my brothers and sisters,
that I have greatly sinned,
in my thoughts and in my words,
in what I have done
and in what I have failed to do,

*Gently strike your chest with a closed fist.*

through my fault, through my fault,
through my most grievous fault;

*Continue:*

therefore I ask blessed Mary ever-Virgin,
all the Angels and Saints,
and you, my brothers and sisters,
to pray for me to the Lord our God.

**Leader:** May almighty God have mercy on us, forgive us
our sins, and bring us to everlasting life.

**All:** **Amen.**

# Listen to God's Word

Reader: A reading from the holy Gospel according to Mark.

*Read Mark 1:1–8.*
The Gospel of the Lord.

All: **Praise to you, Lord Jesus Christ.**

# Dialogue

How did John tell the people to prepare for the coming of the Messiah?

What does it mean to repent?

## Raise Hands in Prayer

*Sit before the wreath in silence and reflect on ways you will try to change your heart.*

Leader: Lord, we want your Spirit to change our hearts and prepare for your coming. Be with us as we pray.

*Stand, raise your hands, and pray the Lord's Prayer.*

Leader: Let us offer one another a greeting of peace as a sign of our desire to change our hearts.

*All exchange a sign of peace.*

# Go Forth!

Leader: Let us go forth to prepare the way of the Lord.

All: **Thanks be to God.**

# The Path of Love

John told the people who were waiting for the Messiah that they would have to change. He said, "Prepare the way of the Lord, make straight his paths" (*Mark 1:3*).

**❓ What changes can you make that will straighten your path and bring you closer to Jesus?**

## ACTIVITY
## Show Your Love

Make a coupon book of loving actions you can do for members of your family. You might include things like reading a book to a younger sibling, washing the dog without complaining, cleaning up your room, or taking someone's turn doing the dishes. Give one person in your family a coupon each day this week.

# God's Greatest Gift

The Church's Season of Christmas begins with the Mass of Christmas Eve on December 24 and continues for almost three weeks. The feast of Epiphany comes in the middle of the Christmas season. The season ends in January with the feast of the Baptism of the Lord, the Sunday after Epiphany.

The word *Epiphany* means "showing forth." On Epiphany the Church remembers the visit of the three magi, often called wise men, to the infant Jesus.

The magi came from distant lands, followed a bright star to find the infant Jesus, honored him, and gave glory to God. Epiphany celebrates the belief that Jesus came to earth to save everyone.

## Precious Gifts

To honor the Savior and show him reverence, the magi brought him gifts of gold, frankincense, and myrrh. The gift of gold, a precious metal, showed that they thought of Jesus as worthy of the highest honor. Frankincense, an incense with a pleasing smell, represented the holiness of Jesus. Myrrh is a symbol of preserving and saving. This gift was a sign that Jesus would die for the salvation of all people.

❓ **What gifts of reverence and worship can you offer Jesus?**

# Celebrate Christmas

## Gather

*Pray the Sign of the Cross together.*

**Leader:** Blessed be the name of the Lord.

**All:** **Now and forever.**

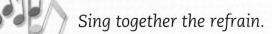

*Sing together the refrain.*

O star of wonder, star of night,
Star with royal beauty bright,
Westward leading, still proceeding,
Guide us to thy perfect Light.

"We Three Kings of Orient Are" Traditional

**Leader:** Let us pray.

*Bow your heads as the leader prays.*

**All:** **Amen.**

## Listen to God's Word

**Reader:** A reading from the holy Gospel according to Matthew.

*Read Matthew 2:9–11.*
The Gospel of the Lord.

**All:** **Praise to you, Lord Jesus Christ.**

# Dialogue

Why did the Magi honor the child Jesus?

How do you honor Jesus today?

## Procession of Gifts

Leader:  May all kings bow before him,
         all nations serve him.

*Psalm 72:11*

All:     **Every nation will adore you.**

*Sing as you walk in procession, carrying the statues of the three kings. Place the statues and your Christmas promises in the crèche.*

# Go Forth!

Leader:  Let us go forth to bring the Christmas gifts of peace, love, and joy to all we meet.

All:     **Thanks be to God.**

*Sing together the refrain.*

O star of wonder, star of night,
Star with royal beauty bright,
Westward leading, still proceeding,
Guide us to thy perfect Light.

"We Three Kings of Orient Are" Traditional

# Gifts from Jesus

The star led the magi to Jesus. They worshipped Jesus, the light of the world, bringing him gifts for a king. The gifts given to Jesus, he gives to you. By becoming one of us, Jesus brought all people the opportunity to be saved (myrrh), to be holy (frankincense), and to be honored (gold).

**?** **In what ways have you seen Jesus' gifts of salvation, holiness, and dignity at work in the world?**

## (ACTIVITY)
## Make a Group Mural

Make a group mural titled "Gifts for All." Draw a way that you will bring the message of Jesus to others in the weeks ahead.

# Called to Leadership

The Church celebrates the feasts of many saints during Ordinary Time. The feast of the conversion of Saint Paul highlights an important event in his life and in the life of the Church. The Church celebrates Saint Paul's conversion on January 25.

## A Change of Heart

Paul was born a Jew in Jesus' time. His Jewish name was Saul. Paul was a faithful Jew, and he worried as he watched the growth in numbers of Jesus' followers after Jesus' death. He saw these disciples as a threat to his traditional Jewish beliefs. Paul began bringing them to the authorities in order to arrest them.

Everything changed when Paul met Jesus on the road to Damascus. He was traveling there to punish some Christians. Instead he experienced the Risen Christ in a vision. Jesus said to him, "Saul, Saul, why are you persecuting me?" (Acts 22:7). After that Paul changed his ways.

Paul became a central figure in the growth of the early Church. Because he met the Risen Christ as the Apostles did, he is called an Apostle, too. His missionary journeys, his many letters, and the power of his preaching helped Christianity to spread far and wide in the world.

❓ **What are some ways your parish preaches the good news?**

# Celebrate Paul

## Gather

*Pray the Sign of the Cross together.*

Leader: Our help is in the name of the Lord.

All: **Who made heaven and earth.**

*Sing together the refrain.*

All grownups, all children,
   all mothers, all fathers
Are sisters and brothers in the family of God.

"All Grownups, All Children" © 1997, GIA Publications, Inc.

Leader: Let us pray.

*Bow your heads as the leader prays.*

All: **Amen.**

## Listen to God's Word

Reader: A reading from the Acts of the Apostles.

*Read Acts 9:19b–22.*
The word of the Lord.

All: **Thanks be to God.**

## Dialogue

How did Paul change as a result of meeting the Risen Christ?

What gifts did Saint Paul bring to the Church?

## Signing of the Senses

*Step forward one by one as the leader signs your eyes, lips, and hands with the cross of salvation. After each person is signed, say the following.*

All:  **Christ will be your strength!**
      **Learn to know and follow him!**

GIA Publications

*After the signing of the senses, bow your head as the leader prays.*

Leader:  Lord Jesus, we place ourselves entirely under the sign of your cross, in the name of the Father, and of the Son, and of the Holy Spirit.

All:  **Amen.**

# Go Forth!

Leader:  Let us go forth in the spirit of Saint Paul to bring the message of Jesus to all.

All:  **Thanks be to God.**

# The Help of the Holy Spirit

Saint Paul knew his weakness, and prayed that the Holy Spirit would give him the gifts he needed to share the message of Jesus with others. You are called to do the same. Sometimes it will be easy, and sometimes it may be very difficult. But the Holy Spirit is always with you.

❓ **In what ways can you lead others to know the good news of Jesus?**

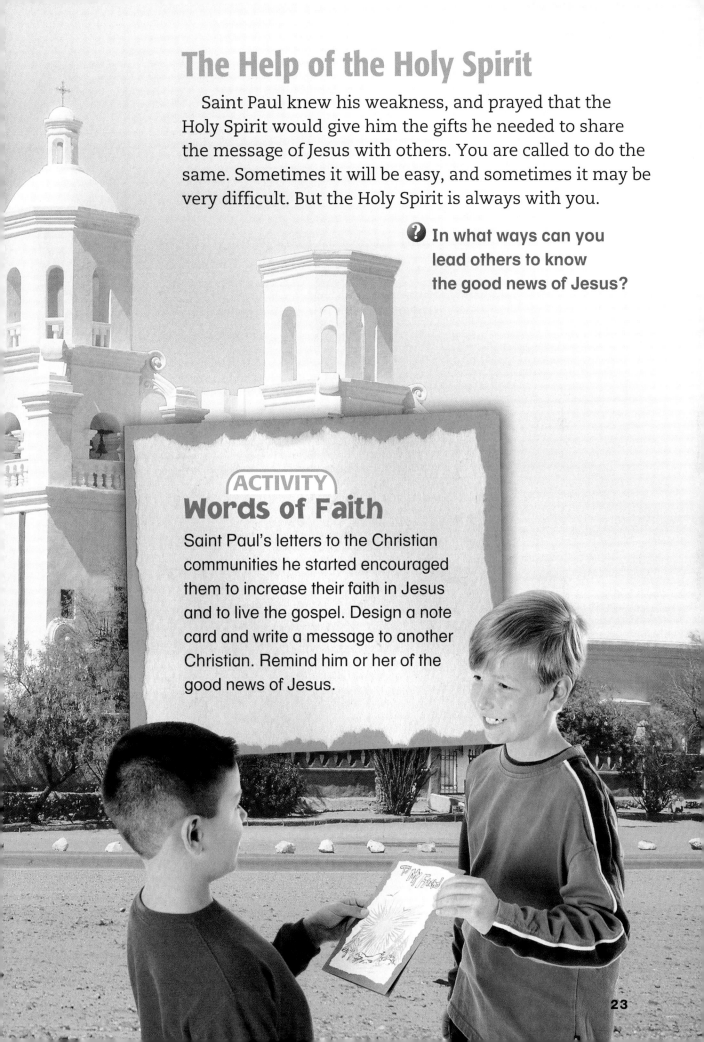

## ⌒ACTIVITY⌒
## Words of Faith

Saint Paul's letters to the Christian communities he started encouraged them to increase their faith in Jesus and to live the gospel. Design a note card and write a message to another Christian. Remind him or her of the good news of Jesus.

# An Unselfish Spirit

**T**rees and vines can grow wild when no one takes care of them. They produce sour fruit or fruit too small to enjoy. That is why it is important to prune trees and vines. *Pruning* means cutting off dead and unhealthy branches so that the best fruit can grow. Trees and vines also require plenty of soil, water, and sunlight.

## Spiritual Discipline

During the Season of Lent, the Church reminds you that good pruning is needed to produce good fruit. As a follower of Jesus, you can produce good fruit by cutting away bad habits and selfishness. Then the good fruit of love, sharing, and forgiveness can grow in you.

Prayer, fasting, and almsgiving are the three principal practices of Lent. These are the practices of disciples of Jesus. Prayer is the foundation for all spiritual discipline. It is like the soil a tree needs to grow. It gives you spiritual nourishment and deepens your relationship with God.

❓ **What are some things you can prune away to grow as a follower of Jesus?**

# Celebrate Lent

## Gather

*Sing together.*

O Lord, hear my prayer,
O Lord, hear my prayer:
when I call answer me.
O Lord, hear my prayer,
O Lord, hear my prayer,
Come and listen to me.

"O Lord, Hear My Prayer" © 1982, Les Presses de Taizé,
GIA Publications, Inc., agent

*Pray the Sign of the Cross together.*

**Leader:** Oh Lord, open my lips.

**All:** **That my mouth shall proclaim your praise.**

**Leader:** Let us pray.

*Raise your hands as the leader prays.*

**All:** **Amen.**

## Listen to God's Word

**Reader:** A reading from the holy Gospel according to Matthew.

*Read Matthew 6:5–8.*
The Gospel of the Lord.

**All:** **Praise to you, Lord Jesus Christ.**

## Dialogue

Why does Jesus say that it is better to pray in secret?

How can prayer help you to yield "good fruit"?

### Kneel in Silence

*Quietly ask God to strengthen you to turn toward his love and to be faithful to the gospel.*

## Prayer of the Faithful

Leader:  God does not desire our death but rather that we should turn from our sins and have life. Let us pray that we may sin no more and so bear good fruit.

*Respond to each prayer with these words.*

All:  **Lord, hear our prayer.**

## Go Forth!

Leader:  Lord, may our Lenten prayer strengthen us so that we may bear good fruit and be good news.

All:  **Thanks be to God.**

# Growing Spiritually

Your body is growing every day. Growing in spirit is equally important. Just as you feed your body, so must your soul be fed. The spiritual discipline of prayer strengthens you so that you can avoid sin and prepare for the joy of Easter.

❓ **What habits of prayer do you already have?**

❓ **What is your plan for strengthening your life of prayer during this Lent?**

## ACTIVITY
## On Good Soil

On a separate piece of paper, draw a tree and its roots. Beneath the roots of the tree, list six ways you could try to deepen your life of prayer during Lent. Try one way during each of the six weeks of Lent.

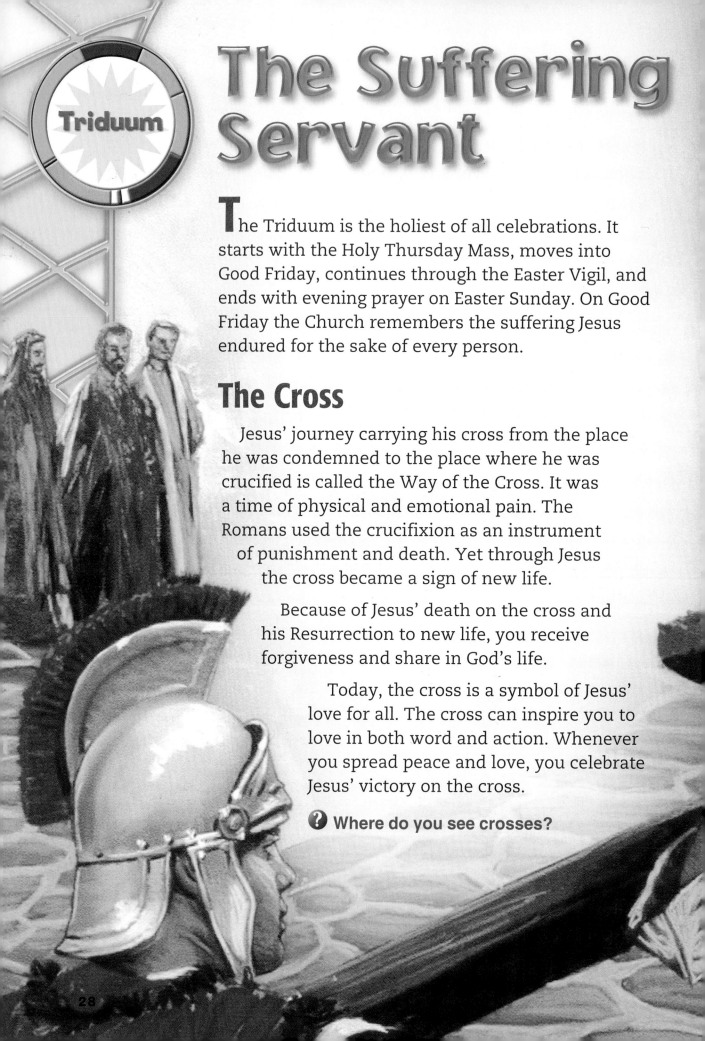

# The Suffering Servant

**T**he Triduum is the holiest of all celebrations. It starts with the Holy Thursday Mass, moves into Good Friday, continues through the Easter Vigil, and ends with evening prayer on Easter Sunday. On Good Friday the Church remembers the suffering Jesus endured for the sake of every person.

## The Cross

Jesus' journey carrying his cross from the place he was condemned to the place where he was crucified is called the Way of the Cross. It was a time of physical and emotional pain. The Romans used the crucifixion as an instrument of punishment and death. Yet through Jesus the cross became a sign of new life.

Because of Jesus' death on the cross and his Resurrection to new life, you receive forgiveness and share in God's life.

Today, the cross is a symbol of Jesus' love for all. The cross can inspire you to love in both word and action. Whenever you spread peace and love, you celebrate Jesus' victory on the cross.

❓ **Where do you see crosses?**

# Celebrate Triduum

## Gather

*Pray the Sign of the Cross together.*

**Leader:** O Lord, open my lips.

**All:** **That my mouth may proclaim your praise.**

*Sing together.*

O how good is Christ the Lord!
On the cross he died for me.
In three days he rose again. Glory be to Jesus!
Glory be to Jesus! Glory be to Jesus!
In three days he rose again. Glory be to Jesus!

"O How Good Is Christ the Lord" Puerto Rican traditional

**Leader:** Let us pray.

*Bow your heads as the leader prays.*

**All:** **Amen.**

## Listen to God's Word

**Reader:** A reading from the Book of the prophet Isaiah.

*Read Isaiah 53:10b–12.*
The word of the Lord.

**All:** **Thanks be to God.**

## Dialogue

The Book of Isaiah was written long before the birth of Jesus. Why do you think the Church reads this passage on Good Friday?

## Prayer of the Faithful

*After each prayer, kneel for a moment in silent prayer, then stand as the leader prays.*

### Honor the Cross

Leader:  This is the wood of the cross,
on which hung the Savior of the world.

All:  **Come. Let us worship.**

*Stand and say the following acclamation three times, bowing deeply first to the left, then to the right, then to the center, always facing the cross.*

All:  **Holy is God!**
**Holy and Strong!**

*Step forward in silence, one by one, and reverence the cross by bowing, kissing the cross, or offering some other sign of reverence.*

# Go Forth!

Leader:  Confessing that Jesus is Lord to the glory of God, go forth in the peace of Christ.

All:  **Thanks be to God.**

*Depart in silence.*

# New Life

The passage from the Book of Isaiah was written long before Jesus was born. Isaiah told the people that someday one of God's servants would suffer for the sins of many. Jesus suffered and died to free all people from sin and to bring them back to God's friendship. That is why the Church calls Jesus the Suffering Servant.

**?** **What are some ways you can imitate the love of Jesus in word and action?**

## ACTIVITY

## A Flower Cross

Make flower petals out of art paper or colored tissue. Write on the flower petals some act of kindness or sacrifice that you will do during the Triduum. Glue the flowers onto a cardboard cross. Let your flower-cross be a reminder of your faith that the way of the cross leads to life.

# Light of the World

**O**n Easter the Church celebrates Jesus' Resurrection. When Jesus was raised from the dead on the third day, he conquered the power of sin and death. The Church celebrates Easter for fifty days from Easter Sunday to Pentecost.

The Easter season is one of joy and gladness. Alleluias are sung once again. Flowers and plants fill the churches, signs of the new life Christ brings. Choirs sing Glory to God! and the altar is draped in white cloth. All are signs of the light that Jesus brings into the world.

## Light in the Darkness

In the northern hemisphere, Easter comes at a time when the darkness of winter has given way to spring. Leaves appear on trees and flowers blossom. Spring is a season of new life.

Jesus' Resurrection is a sign of the new life that bursts forth in the bright light of the sun. Jesus triumphed over the selfishness that leads people away from God. He turned the darkness of sin into the light of love. That is why Jesus is called the Light of the World.

❓ **What are some ways Jesus is light for you?**

# Celebrate Easter

## Gather

*Pray the Sign of the Cross together.*

**Leader:** Light and peace in Jesus Christ our Lord. Alleluia.

**All:** **Thanks be to God, alleluia.**

**Reader:** Christ is our light in the darkness!

**All:** **Alleluia, alleluia, alleluia.**

**Reader:** Christ shows us the path of love and light!

**All:** **Alleluia, alleluia, alleluia.**

**Reader:** Christ is the Way, the Truth, and the Life!

**All:** **Alleluia, alleluia, alleluia.**

**Leader:** Let us pray.

*Bow your heads as the leader prays.*

**All:** **Amen, Alleluia.**

## Listen to God's Word

**Reader:** A reading from the holy Gospel according to Matthew.

*Read Matthew 28:1–10.*
The Gospel of the Lord.

**All:** **Praise to you, Lord Jesus Christ.**

## Dialogue

What was your first thought as you heard this gospel?

What did Jesus tell the women?

## Blessing with Holy Water

*Step forward and bow before the Easter candle. Then dip your hand in the blessed water and make the Sign of the Cross.*

Sing together the refrain.

Alleluia, alleluia, alleluia!

"Easter Alleluia" © 1986, GIA Publications, Inc.

**Leader:** Let us pray.

*Bow your head as the leader prays.*

**All:**    **Amen.**

# Go Forth!

**Leader:** Let us go forth and share the good news that Christ our light has risen! Alleluia!

**All:**    **Thanks be to God. Alleluia!**

# Let Your Light Shine

Did you ever notice that outside on a dark night, away from the lights of the city, the stars seem brighter? In a similar way, the light of Christ brightens the darkness of the world. In the midst of sadness and violence, Christ's light shines even more brightly. In the midst of loneliness or rejection, the light of Christ's love is there to warm the heart that is hurting.

**❓ What are some things you can do to help others to know the light of Christ's love?**

(ACTIVITY)

## The Light of the World

On poster board, make a Christ candle. Decorate your candle with symbols of Jesus as the Light of the World. Draw seven rays of light radiating from the candle flame. On the rays write things you and your family can do each week during the Easter season to bring Christ's light into your neighborhood and community. Share your ideas with your family.

# The Power of the Holy Spirit

The Feast of Pentecost is one of the most important celebrations of the Church. The Acts of the Apostles tell us that the followers of Jesus were gathered in Jerusalem fifty days after Easter when the Holy Spirit came to them.

## Pentecost Today

Today the Church rejoices in the Resurrection of the Lord for fifty days after Easter. Then on Pentecost, the Church celebrates the gift of the Holy Spirit to the Church. The Holy Spirit gave the first disciples the wisdom and courage they needed to preach the gospel.

The coming of the Holy Spirit marked the true beginning of the Church. From this time onward, the Church has been empowered by the Holy Spirit to spread the good news by word and action. He builds up the Church, empowers her for service, and is the source of her holiness.

**❓ How is the Holy Spirit active in the world today?**

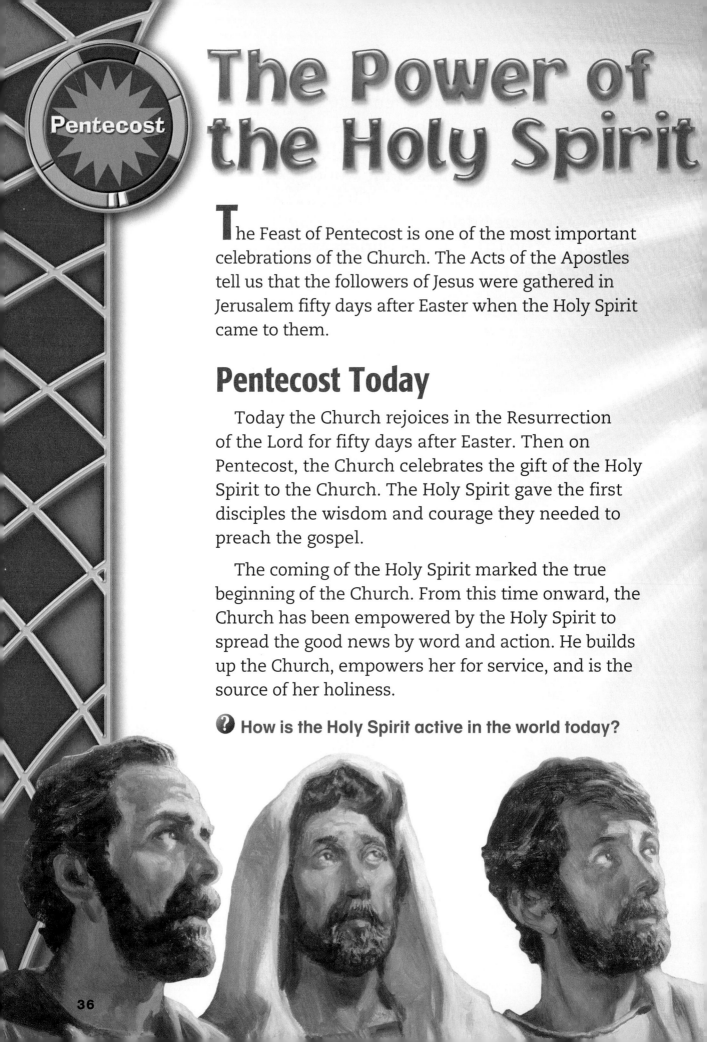

# Celebrate Pentecost

## Gather

*Pray the Sign of the Cross together.*

**Leader:** Light and peace in Jesus Christ our Lord, alleluia.

**All:** **Thanks be to God, alleluia.**

*Sing together.*

If you believe and I believe,
And we together pray,
The Holy Spirit must come down
And set God's people free,
And set God's people free,
And set God's people free;
The Holy Spirit must come down
And set God's people free.

"If You Believe and I Believe" © 1991, GIA Publications, Inc.

**Leader:** Let us pray.

*Bow your heads as the leader prays.*

**All:** **Amen.**

## Listen to God's Word

**Reader:** A reading from the Acts of the Apostles.

*Read Acts 2:1–11.*
The word of the Lord.

**All:** **Thanks be to God.**

## Dialogue

What are three things that happened to the disciples because of the coming of the Holy Spirit?

How can the Holy Spirit strengthen you?

### Offering of Gifts

*Sing together, "If You Believe and I Believe." As you sing, come forward in procession and place gifts for the poor at the base of the prayer table.*

### Prayer of the Faithful

Leader:  Let us pray for the Church and the world, that all will be open to the power of the Holy Spirit.

*Respond to each prayer with these words.*

All:  **Send us your Spirit, O Lord.**

# Go Forth!

Leader:  May God bless us and give us the gifts of the Holy Spirit forever. And let us go forth in love and service to all God's people, alleluia.

All:  **Thanks be to God, alleluia!**

# Gifts of the Holy Spirit

Many stories in the Acts of the Apostles tell how the Holy Spirit guided the followers of Jesus to spread the Good News of Jesus. The disciples told all who would listen about the life of Jesus and his commandment of love. But they lived the way of Jesus as well. You are called to do the same today.

At Baptism you received the gifts of the Holy Spirit— wisdom, understanding, right judgment, courage, knowledge, reverence, and fear of the Lord. In Confirmation you will be strengthened with these gifts.

**When has the Holy Spirit helped you to use one of these gifts?**

**(ACTIVITY)**
## The Holy Spirit

Read one of the Scripture stories that describe the work of the early Church. With a small group, act out this story for the rest of your class. Tell how the story shows the presence of the Holy Spirit.

Acts 4:32–35

Acts 6:1–7

Acts 9:26–31

# Unit 1
# Revelation

**In this unit you will...**

learn that God communicates a loving plan for all of creation. We learn of this in Scripture and Tradition. God stays true and faithful to his promises. Through his covenants, God keeps telling and showing people that he will be faithful, even though we sin. He helps us understand how to be faithful to him. Through the Ten Commandments, God revealed how he wants all of his children to live.

Chapter 1

Chapter 2

Chapter 3

## Faith in Action!

**Catholic Social Teaching Principle:**
**Care for God's Creation**

# Chapter 1 God's Plan

## Let Us Pray

**Leader:** All-knowing God, we thank you for your guidance.
"I will instruct you and show you the way
you should walk,
give you counsel and watch over you."
*Psalm 32:8*

**All:** All-knowing God, we thank you for your guidance. Amen.

## Activity — Let's Begin

● **Kaleidoscope**   Have you ever looked through a kaleidoscope? As you turn the tube, small bits of colored glass or plastic at the far end are reflected in two mirrors. As you turn the kaleidoscope, the colored bits arrange themselves into thousands of beautiful patterns.

Write a haiku—a type of poem—about the beauty of the kaleidoscope patterns on this page.

_____

_____

_____

_____

_____

● **Make a Kaleidoscope Pattern**   On a separate sheet of paper, make your own kaleidoscope pattern.

# God's Creation

**Focus** What did God say about all that he had made?

The world is something like a kaleidoscope. Its complex patterns and movements give clues to God's amazing plan for creation. In this poem the poet imagines a powerful God who walks and talks like a man. Read to learn how the poet thinks God feels about creation.

A POEM

## The Creation

. . . And far as the eye of God could see
Darkness covered everything.
Blacker than a hundred midnights
Down in a cypress swamp.

Then God smiled,
And the light broke,
And the darkness rolled up on one side,
And the light stood shining on the other,
And God said: "That's good!"

Then God reached out and took the light
in his hands,
And God rolled the light around in his hands
Until he made the sun;
And he set that sun a-blazing in the heavens.
And the light that was left from making the sun
God gathered it up in a shining ball
And flung it against the darkness,
Spangling the night with the moon and stars.
Then down between
The darkness and the light
He hurled the world;
And God said: "That's good!"

*Then God made the seven seas and all the forests and plants and animals and even rainbows. But God decided to make even more.*

Then God sat down—
On the side of a hill where he could think;
By a deep, wide river he sat down;
With his head in his hands,
God thought and thought,
Till he thought: I'll make me a man!

Up from the bed of the river
God scooped the clay;
And by the bank of the river
He kneeled him down;
And there the great God Almighty
Who lit the sun and fixed it in the sky,
Who flung the stars to the most far corner of the night,
Who rounded the earth in the middle of his hand;
This great God,
Like a mammy bending over her baby,
Kneeled down in the dust
Toiling over a lump of clay
Till he shaped it in his own image;

Then into it he blew the breath of life,
And man became a living soul.

From the poem by James Weldon Johnson

**❓ What did you learn about God from this poem?**

## Activity　Share Your Faith

**Reflect:** In what ways does the world show God's love and care for his creation?

**Share:** With a partner, name some of these ways.

**Act:** Make a scenic postcard design of one part of the world that shows God's love and care.

# God's Plan

 **Focus** Where does God reveal his plan for you?

## Faith Fact

The ancient town of Nineveh is located near the Tigris River in present-day Iraq.

God has a loving plan for creation. As God's plan unfolds, he keeps everyone and everything in his loving care. This is called **providence**. In this Bible story from the Old Testament, you will learn about Jonah, a man who tried to avoid God's plan for him.

✝ **SCRIPTURE**                    **Book of Jonah**

## Jonah and the Big Fish

God told Jonah to tell the people of Nineveh, "The Lord has seen your sins. Change your sinful ways, or you are doomed!" Jonah got on a ship and sailed away to hide from the Lord.

God made a storm come up, and the ship was about to be broken to pieces. The sailors ran and found Jonah sleeping. "Pray to your God, that he may save us!" they cried. Jonah thought that God was punishing him, so he asked the sailors to throw him into the sea. As soon as they did, the sea became calm.

The Lord sent a giant fish that swallowed Jonah. Inside the fish, Jonah had some time to think, and he decided to follow the Lord. Three days later the fish spit him onto dry land. God was merciful to Jonah and also to the people of Nineveh, who listened to Jonah and changed their ways.

Based on the Book of Jonah

❓ **Why do you think Jonah tried to run from God?**

❓ **Have you ever avoided doing something that you knew you should do? What happened?**

## Following God's Plan

The story of Jonah is in the Old Testament of the Bible. The Bible, also called **Scripture**, is God's word written in human words. There are many more stories in the Old Testament that can show you how others have followed God's plan. Then, in the New Testament, you can see God's Son, Jesus, answering his Father's call perfectly. Through Jesus you can learn how you are to respond to God's plan for you. The Holy Spirit, whom Jesus sent to the Church, will help you.

## God's Revelation

God has made himself known gradually throughout history by words and deeds and the experience of people. The truth that God has told the world about himself is called **revelation**. Revelation is found in Scripture and in the Tradition of the Church.

❓ **What did Jonah do to figure out how to fit into God's plan for him?**

❓ **What do you think is God's plan for you?**

## Activity — Connect Your Faith

**Your Best Thinking** Think about quiet and beautiful places you have seen on a nature program or on another TV show. Draw in the TV screen a peaceful place where you could spend time thinking about important things. Then imagine yourself in this place, and think about God's plan for you.

# Space for Prayer

 **Focus** Where do you pray?

Prayer helps you learn about God's plan for you. Quiet time and a special place make it easier to think and pray. A prayer space is a place you can go to feel close to God.

## Make Your Own Space

### 1. Find a Space

Think of a quiet place where you will not be disturbed. The space needs to be a place that you have permission to use and can get to by yourself. It can be in your home, your yard, or any place where you will feel safe.

### 2. Prepare the Space

After you choose a prayer space, decide how you want to prepare it. If you are indoors, you might want to close the curtains or blinds, allowing only soft light. Perhaps you would like to add a religious picture, a cross, or an object from nature to help you quiet your mind and focus.

### 3. Prepare Yourself

Be sure to prepare yourself for prayer. Focus your eyes and listen to your breathing. Remember that God breathed his life into you when you were created. Think about a story of Jesus from the Bible, or imagine that he is sitting with you.

### 4. Pray

Pray from your heart. Listen for God. Give thanks to him for his constant presence in your life. If you start to think of something else, remind yourself that this is a time for prayer.

❓ **Where do you have or would you like to have your prayer space?**

# Live Your Faith

**Write a Quieting Prayer**   A quieting prayer is a phrase that you can repeat to quiet your mind. Some examples are, "Jesus, be my guide" and "God, teach me your path of goodness." Write your ideas in the space below.

_____

_____

_____

_____

**Draw Your Prayer Space**   In the space provided, draw a picture of you in your prayer space. Be sure to include everything that is important to your space.

# Psalm of Hope

 **Let Us Pray**

*Gather and begin with the Sign of the Cross.*

*Sing together the refrain.*

Guiding me, guarding me, the Lord is by my side;
guiding me, guarding me, the Lord upholds my life.

"Psalm 121" © 1988, GIA Publications, Inc.

**Leader:** Loving God, hear us today as we pray.

**Group 1:** I raise my eyes toward the mountains.
From where will my help come?
My help comes from the LORD,
the maker of heaven and earth.

**All:** *Sing refrain.*

**Group 2:** God will not allow your foot to slip.
Truly, the guardian of Israel
never slumbers nor sleeps.

**All:** *Sing refrain.*

**The LORD will guard you
from all evil.
The LORD will guard your
coming and going both
now and forever.**

*Sing refrain.*

Based on *Psalm 121*

**Leader:** Let us pray.
*Bow your heads as
the leader prays.*

**All:** **Amen.**

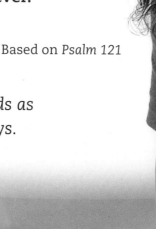

# Chapter 2

# God Is Faithful

## Let Us Pray

**Leader:** Lord, we place our trust in your faithfulness.

"The LORD is trustworthy in every word,
and faithful in every work."

*Psalm 145:13*

**All:** Lord, we place our trust in your faithfulness. Amen.

## Activity — Let's Begin

### A Very Bad Day

My day was going smooth as silk,
'Til the cat leapt up and spilled my milk.
As I was mopping up the floor,
My mom was calling from the door.
"Hurry up! We'll all be late!"
I grabbed the toast left on my plate.
Just as we reached the end of the block,
I noticed I had no left sock.
I got to school five minutes late,
I guess my toast will have to wait.
As I raced inside the classroom door,
My homework lay on the living room floor!

• How can bad days be avoided?

_____

_____

**Write a Skit**  Think about what happened on your last bad day, and write a skit.

# Humans Choose Sin

**Focus** How does God show his faithfulness?

For the first humans, known as Adam and Eve in the Old Testament creation story, there was a time when every day was a good day. But one day Satan, who was God's enemy, came to Eve in the form of a snake and tempted her. We learn from the Book of Genesis what Adam and Eve did.

## ✝ SCRIPTURE                                    Genesis 3

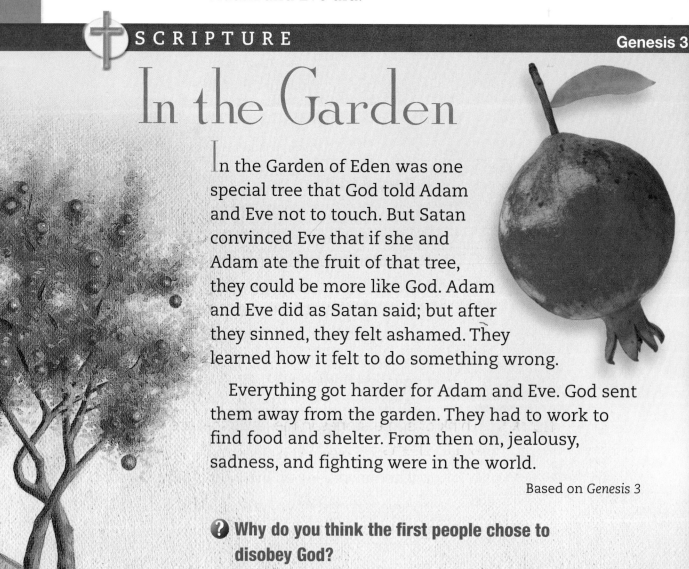

## In the Garden

In the Garden of Eden was one special tree that God told Adam and Eve not to touch. But Satan convinced Eve that if she and Adam ate the fruit of that tree, they could be more like God. Adam and Eve did as Satan said; but after they sinned, they felt ashamed. They learned how it felt to do something wrong.

Everything got harder for Adam and Eve. God sent them away from the garden. They had to work to find food and shelter. From then on, jealousy, sadness, and fighting were in the world.

Based on *Genesis 3*

❓ **Why do you think the first people chose to disobey God?**

# Consequences

Humans were created to share God's life and to be happy with God forever. By disobeying God, the first people broke their friendship with God. This sin of the first humans is called **Original Sin** because since that choice was made, sin has been present throughout the world. Original Sin affects every human. Ignorance, the inclination to sin, suffering, and death all came into the world as a result of Original Sin.

Even though God sent Adam and Eve away from the garden, he did not abandon them. God remained faithful. In return he wanted all humans to be free and faithful to him, so that they could be happy forever.

The Book of Genesis then tells another famous story, the story of Noah. The point of Noah's story is that even when people continued to sin and to disobey God, God was faithful.

## Words of Faith

**Original Sin** is the choice of the first people to disobey God.

## Activity

# Share Your Faith

**Reflect:** Think of some stories in the news that are examples of the effects of Original Sin in the world today.

**Share:** In a small group, talk about ways that people can act as God wants them to act in these situations.

**Act:** Write two examples here.

_____

_____

_____

_____

# God's Plan Revealed

 **Focus** What did God promise to Abram?

After a long time, God called a man named Abram to help humans remain faithful. God revealed his plan to Abram in a new way.

## ✚ SCRIPTURE

**Genesis 12:1–8; 15:1–5; 17:5–9, 15; 21:1–3**

# God Calls Abram

Abram lived long, long ago in an ancient city called Haran. God told Abram to leave his country and much of his family and go to a new land called Canaan. God told Abram, "I will bless you and make your descendants into a great nation." Abram obeyed God. He took his wife Sarai, his brother's son Lot, and all their possessions on the long journey to the new land.

Abram and his family were never alone on their difficult journey. They knew that God was always with them. Every time Abram reached a stop on the journey, he built an altar of thanksgiving to the Lord.

Many years later, after Abram had settled in the land of Canaan, the Lord spoke again to him, saying, "Don't be afraid! I will protect and reward you."

Abram replied, "Lord, you have given me everything I could ask for, except children."

The Lord told Abram, "Look at the sky and count the stars. That is how many descendants you will have."

❓ **What is something you have been asked to do that was very hard?**

# God's Covenant with Abraham

God appeared to Abram again. God made a **covenant** with Abram and his descendants for all time. God told Abram that the land of Canaan would belong to Abram and his descendants forever. He said that Abram would be the father of many nations and that these people would be God's people. As a sign of the covenant, God changed the names of Abram and his wife Sarai to Abraham and Sarah. Soon after that, even though Sarah was old, she had a son, whom the couple named Isaac.

Based on *Genesis 12:1–8, 15:1–5, 17:5–9, 15; 21:1–3*

❓ **How did Abraham and Sarah follow God's will?**

Abraham and Sarah never turned away from God. Like Abraham and Sarah, you are **faithful** to God every time you obey his laws and make loving choices.

## Common Ancestors

Abraham is considered an ancestor in faith of Christianity, Judaism, and Islam. These religions see their origins in Abraham's free response to God's revelation that he was the one God they should believe in and follow.

## Words of Faith

A **covenant** is a sacred promise or agreement between God and humans.

To be **faithful** is to be steadfast and loyal in your commitment to God, just as he is faithful to you.

## Activity    Connect Your Faith

**Show Faith**   Write your first name in colorful letters. Around your name, write words that tell how you show that you are faithful to God.

55

# Remain Faithful

 **Focus** How do you remain faithful?

In your prayers, you often ask God for help and guidance. Sometimes his help does not come as quickly as you would like. It may be difficult to be faithful.

Abraham and Sarah prayed and waited for many years before they had their first child. Their son, Isaac, arrived according to the timing of God's plan.

At other times God's answer is not easy to see. Many times when you ask for his help, God gives you the ability to help yourself. Jessica learns this in the following situation.

Jessica wanted the red bicycle she saw at the store. She prayed to ask God for the red bicycle. She continued to pray for several weeks, but still she did not get the bike. One day her neighbor offered Jessica $5 to water his plants while he was out of town. Another neighbor asked Jessica to walk her dog. At the end of the week Jessica had $10. She realized that she could save her money for the bike. With her parents' permission, Jessica started asking neighbors whether they had odd jobs for her to do. After two months, Jessica had enough money to buy the red bicycle.

❓ **When have you asked God for help and later realized that he has given you what you need to help yourself?**

❓ **What are some ways to be faithful as you learn more about God's plan?**

# Live Your Faith

**Look for God's Help** Look at the pictures on this page. On the lines below each picture, write how God-given abilities can help you achieve the result shown. In the blank box, draw a picture of something that you prayed for. On the lines below the box, write how God helped you.

_____

_____

_____

_____

_____

# Prayer for Mercy

 Let Us Pray

*Gather and begin with the Sign of the Cross.*

 *Sing together the refrain.*

God ever-faithful,
God ever-merciful,
God of your people,
hear our prayer.

"General Intercessions" © 1990,
GIA Publications, Inc.

**Leader:**     For times we have failed,
we pray,

**All:**     *Sing refrain.*

**Reader 1:**     For people in the world
who have been hurt
by our neglect,
we pray,

**All:**     *Sing refrain.*

**Reader 2:**     For times when we were
unfaithful to God's
covenant of love,
we pray,

**All:**     *Sing refrain.*

**Leader:**     Let us pray.

*Bow your heads as
the leader prays.*

**All:**     **Amen.**

**A** **Work with Words**   Complete each sentence with the correct word from the Word Bank.

**WORD BANK**

faithful
sin
Exodus
covenant
hope
names
friendship

1.  By disobeying God, the first people broke their
    _____ with him.

2.  One consequence of the disobedience of Adam
    and Eve is the inclination to _____.

3.  God always remains _____ to
    his people.

4.  God made a _____ with Abraham and
    his descendants.

5.  As a sign of the covenant, God changed the
    _____ of Abram and Sarai.

**B** **Check Understanding**   Circle the letter of the choice
that best completes each sentence.

6.  God created humans to be _____ with him forever.

    **a.** happy      **b.** confused      **c.** out of relationship

7.  _____ is the child of Abraham and Sarah.

    **a.** Adam      **b.** Isaac      **c.** Eve

**C** **Make Connections**   Write one thing you have learned about God from
each of the following stories.

8.  In the Garden _____

    _____

9.  God Calls Abram _____

    _____

10. Sign of the Covenant _____

    _____

# Family Faith

## Catholics Believe

- God's covenant with Abraham reveals that God is always faithful to his people.

- Sin is present in the world because of human choice.

### SCRIPTURE

Read *Genesis 13*, *Genesis 21:1–8*, or *Genesis 25:7–11* to find other stories about Abraham and Sarah.

**GO online** **www.osvcurriculum.com**
For weekly scripture readings and seasonal resources

## Activity

# Live Your Faith

**Travel Brochure** Share with your family one thing that you learned in class. Then imagine that you could visit the places where Abraham and Sarah traveled. As a family, make pages for a travel brochure that tells about their experiences. Think of the stories in this chapter. Look in a Bible to find a map of Abraham's journey. Bring your brochure to share with the group.

# People of Faith

**Naomi** was an Israelite who, because of a great famine, left her home to live among people of another land. While living in this land, she remained faithful to the God of Israel. When her husband and two sons died, she wanted to return to the land of her ancestors. Her daughter-in-law **Ruth** promised to come with her. Ruth told Naomi, "For wherever you go I will go, wherever you lodge I will lodge, your people shall be my people, and your God my God" (*Ruth 1:16*).

▲ Naomi and Ruth

## Family Prayer

Loving God, please help us remain faithful to our covenant relationship with you, as Ruth and Naomi did. Amen.

# Chapter 3 The Ten Commandments

**Leader:** Loving Father, help us hear your voice and know your will.

"To do your will is my delight;
    my God, your law is in my heart!"

*Psalm 40:9*

**All:** Loving Father, help us hear your voice and know your will. Amen.

## Activity  Let's Begin

● **The Golden Eggs**   There once lived a farmer and his wife who were very poor. One day, a beautiful goose strutted across their path. The woman sighed, "What a beautiful bird!"

The goose followed the couple home. The next morning, they found that the goose had laid a golden egg. Each day the goose laid yet another golden egg. Soon, the couple became rich.

But the farmer grew impatient for more gold. "I will kill the goose and slice her open," he thought, "and I'll have all her eggs at once." So he cut open the goose, but inside there were no more golden eggs. And now he had no goose!

Think about what this story teaches you. Write your idea here. _____

● **Draw a Comic Strip**   Draw a comic strip about the results of one of the choices you made yesterday.

# Journey to Freedom

 **Focus** Who helped lead God's people to freedom?

In the story of "The Golden Eggs," the husband was a slave to greed. Here are two Bible stories about how God led his people from slavery to freedom.

✝ **SCRIPTURE**                    **Genesis 37:1–4, 42:6–8, 44:1–12, 45:4–5**

## Joseph and His Brothers

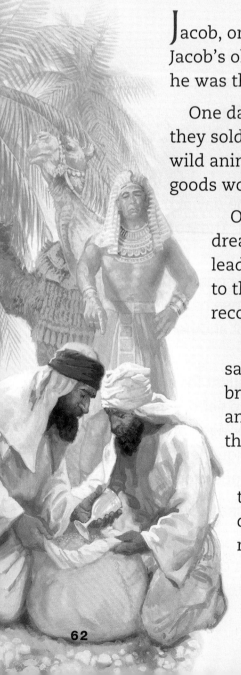

Jacob, one of Abraham's descendants, had twelve sons. Jacob's older sons hated their younger brother Joseph because he was their father's favorite.

One day Joseph's brothers threw him into a dry well. Then they sold him as a slave in Egypt. They told their father that wild animals had killed Joseph. Now more of their father's goods would belong to them.

Over the years, Joseph's power to tell the meaning of dreams won him a place of honor with Pharaoh, the leader of Egypt. During a famine, Joseph's brothers came to the court to beg for grain. The brothers did not recognize Joseph, but Joseph knew them.

To test them, Joseph had servants fill the brothers' sacks with grain and put a silver cup into the sack of his brother Benjamin. Later he had his servants follow them and discover the silver cup in the sack. Joseph then told the brothers that Benjamin was to be his slave.

Benjamin's brother Judah pleaded for him, saying that their father would be brokenhearted if Benjamin did not return. At this news, Joseph wept and told the men that he was their brother. He forgave them.

Based on *Genesis 37:1–4, 42:6–8, 44:1–12, 45:4–5*

❓ **When have you forgiven someone as Joseph did?**

## From Slavery to Freedom

When Joseph's brothers sold him as a slave, they caused problems for themselves as well. It was only when Joseph forgave his brothers that his family knew real freedom and happiness again.

✝ SCRIPTURE                    Exodus 2:1–10, 14:10–31, 15:19–21

# The Exodus from Egypt

Many years later God's people, the Israelites, were slaves in Egypt. Their male children were being killed, so one Israelite mother hid her baby boy in a basket near the Nile River. When Pharaoh's daughter found the baby, she kept him and named him Moses. She raised him at court as her son.

When Moses grew older, God called him to be a leader of his people. God asked Moses to tell Pharaoh to stop hurting the Israelites, but Pharaoh did not listen.

Finally, Moses was able to lead the Israelites out of Egypt. At the Red Sea, Moses raised his staff and the waters parted for the Israelites to pass through.

*Based on Exodus 2:1–10, 14:10–31, 15:19–21*

❓ **Do you think it was hard for Moses to leave Pharaoh's court? Why or why not?**

## Activity  Share Your Faith

**Reflect:** When have you been jealous of someone else because of his or her gifts or belongings?

**Share:** Tell a partner why you were jealous of this person and how you handled the situation.

**Act:** Imagine that you are writing a musical, and use a familiar tune to help you write a song that explains the situation.

63

# A Guide from God

 **Focus** How do the Ten Commandments help you be free?

The Israelites were free from slavery, but they still needed God's help.

## ✝ SCRIPTURE
Exodus 17—20

# The Journey Continues

# Words of Faith

The **Ten Commandments** are the summary of laws that God gave Moses on Mount Sinai. They tell what is necessary in order to love God and others.

After the Israelites crossed the Red Sea, they wandered in the desert for years. They forgot that God had saved them from slavery in Egypt. Moses struggled to keep order among God's people and to find food and water for them. He complained to God about his hard job, and God helped him.

In the desert, God called Moses up to Mount Sinai. After God showed his power with thunder and lightning, he gave Moses the **Ten Commandments** to show the people how they were to live.

*Based on Exodus 17—20*

**❓ Why do you think the Ten Commandments are important?**

## Living God's Covenant

Just as the Ten Commandments helped the Israelites live their covenant relationship with God, the commandments are also a guide for you. They tell you the minimum that is required to love God and others. The first three commandments show you how to be faithful to God. The last seven show you how to treat other people with love. The chart on the next page names the Ten Commandments and explains what each one means for you.

# The Ten Commandments

| The commandment | What the commandment means |
|---|---|
| 1. I am the Lord your God. You shall not have strange gods before me. | • Place your faith in God alone.<br>• Worship, praise, and thank the Creator.<br>• Believe in, trust, and love God. |
| 2. You shall not take the name of the Lord your God in vain. | • Speak God's name with reverence.<br>• Don't curse.<br>• Never call on God to witness to a lie. |
| 3. Remember to keep holy the Lord's day. | • Gather to worship at the Eucharist.<br>• Rest and avoid unnecessary work on Sunday. |
| 4. Honor your father and your mother. | • Respect and obey your parents, guardians, and others who have proper authority. |
| 5. You shall not kill. | • Respect and protect the lives of others and your own life. |
| 6. You shall not commit adultery. | • Be faithful and loyal to friends and family.<br>• Respect God's gift of sexuality. |
| 7. You shall not steal. | • Respect the things that belong to others.<br>• Share what you have with those in need. |
| 8. You shall not bear false witness against your neighbor. | • Be honest and truthful.<br>• Do not brag about yourself.<br>• Do not say untruthful or negative things about others. |
| 9. You shall not covet your neighbor's wife. | • Practice modesty in thoughts, words, dress, and actions. |
| 10. You shall not covet your neighbor's goods. | • Rejoice in others' good fortune.<br>• Do not be jealous of others' possessions.<br>• Do not be greedy. |

## Activity — Connect Your Faith

**Commandments and You**   This week you made a number of decisions. Write down one decision you made, and tell which commandment you followed when you made that decision.

_____

_____

# Keeping the Ten Commandments

 **Focus** How can you live as the Ten Commandments require?

God gave Moses the Ten Commandments to share with the people. These commandments help Christians live in a way that is pleasing to God. Page 65 lists explanations of living each commandment. Here are some other ways to keep the commandments.

## Ways to Keep the Commandments

**1** Remember that religious holidays, such as Christmas and Easter, are about Jesus, not about gifts and candy.

**2** Do not tell jokes that make fun of God, Jesus, or the Church.

**3** On Sunday, go to Mass and spend time in quiet reflection about your week.

**4** Listen when your parents ask you to do something; don't make them ask you repeatedly.

**5** Do not be cruel to animals.

**6** Follow Jesus' example of respecting himself and his friends.

**7** When someone lends you something, treat it with great care. Always return it in good condition.

**8** Do not gossip.

**9** Behave with decency.

**10** Do not think about money and things all the time.

❓ **What are some other ways that you keep the Ten Commandments?**

# Live Your Faith

**Live by the Commandments**   Look at the pictures on this page, and decide which commandment is not being followed. Write the number of the commandment and then explain what you would do in the situation to honor the commandment.

Then, draw a picture of yourself keeping one commandment.

I swear to God, no one will even notice what you are wearing.

_____

_____

_____

_____

_____

_____

Kelly is so dumb! She got a C- on the last test.

_____

_____

_____

I wish I had Mike's new bike.

_____

_____

_____

**Here I am keeping the _____ commandment.**

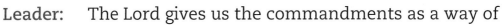

# Psalm of Celebration

 **Let Us Pray**

*Gather and begin with the Sign of the Cross.*

 *Sing together the refrain.*

Sing, O people, sing our God together,
raise your voices: sing alleluia!

"Sing Our God Together" © 1993, GIA Publications, Inc.

**Leader:** The Lord gives us the commandments as a way of living. Let us praise God for the gift of salvation.

**Reader 1:** Then was our mouth filled with laughter, on our lips there were songs.

**All:** *Sing refrain.*

**Reader 2:** What marvels the LORD worked for us! Indeed we were glad.

**All:** *Sing refrain.*

**Reader 3:** Those who are sowing in tears will sing when they reap.

**All:** *Sing refrain.*

**Reader 4:** They go out, they go out, full of tears; they come back, they come back, full of song.

**All:** *Sing refrain.*

**Leader:** Let us pray.

*Bow your heads as the leader prays.*

**All:** **Amen.**

Based on *Psalm 126*

Celebrate

**(A) Work with Words**   Match each description in Column 1 with the correct term in Column 2.

**Column 1**

_____ **1.** forgave his brothers

_____ **2.** place of law-giving

_____ **3.** Israelites' place of slavery

_____ **4.** leader of Egypt

_____ **5.** lead Israelites to freedom

**Column 2**

**a.** Moses

**b.** Pharaoh

**c.** Mount Sinai

**d.** Joseph

**e.** Egypt

**(B) Check Understanding**   Circle True if a statement is true, and circle False if a statement is false. Correct any false statements.

**6.** God gave Moses the Ten Commandments on Mount Sinai.

True     False _____

**7.** The third commandment requires you to avoid gossip.

True     False _____

**(C) Make Connections**   Write these commandments, and add one way to keep each of them.

**8. 4th:** _____

_____

_____

**9. 5th:** _____

_____

_____

**10. 7th:** _____

_____

_____

# Family Faith

## Catholics Believe

- God gave you the Ten Commandments to help you be faithful to him and his covenant.

- The commandments tell you ways to love God and others.

### ✝ SCRIPTURE

Read *Matthew 5:43–48* to learn about the importance of loving both friends and enemies.

**GO online** **www.osvcurriculum.com**
For weekly scripture readings and seasonal resources

## Activity
# Live Your Faith

**Covenants** With your family, discuss what you learned about living God's covenant. Then write a family covenant. Begin by writing ways that you will show love and respect for one another. Then, write a promise to love God and others. Sign your names to the covenant, and display it where all can see it.

# People of Faith

**Aaron** was the older brother of Moses. He assisted his brother in the Exodus from Egypt and during the years in the desert. Aaron was a high priest, responsible for the worship and sacrifice that would keep the Israelites on the path God had set for them. **Miriam** was the sister of Aaron and Moses. She is called a prophet—a person who speaks the truth to the people about God. She led the women in song and dance after the escape from Egypt.

▲ Aaron and Miriam
c. 1800 B.C.

## Family Prayer

God our Father, help us see and follow your guidance, as Aaron and Miriam did. Give us patience on our faith journey. Amen.

*In Unit 1 your child is learning about REVELATION.*

**70** CCC *See Catechism of the Catholic Church 2055, 2060–2061 for further reading on chapter content.*

# Faith in Action
## CATHOLIC SOCIAL TEACHING

In this unit you learned that God created the world and everything in it. He loves and cares for all that he made, and he has a plan for the world. You are one of his people, and you are part of that plan. The Ten Commandments are rules God gave that tell you how to live together. They call you to love God and to treat other people with love.

## Care for Creation

After God created the world and the people in it, he asked humans to care for creation. You show that you care for creation by taking care of resources such as land and plants and by using them well. This is a way to thank God for the many gifts he has given you.

Humans are part of creation, too. In fact, humans are a very special part of creation because God created people in his image. When you take care of other people and treat them with love, you are doing your part in God's plan. Helping other people shows that you recognize his creation of human life as a special and precious gift.

? **How can you show that you care for God's creation?**

# More Than Just a Garden

**G**od asks humans to care for his creations. Let's see how one community used God's gift of plants to help others.

**W**hat if one group of people loved to garden and another group did not have enough to eat? How could these two groups connect?

St. Francis of Assisi, a parish in Michigan, began a garden in an unused field. Late in April a group of people came with shovels and prepared the soil for planting. The next week another group spent all day planting seedlings—beans, beets, lettuce, peppers, and strawberries. Adults and children watered the plants, checked for insects, and weeded the plants every day but Sunday.

As soon as the vegetables ripened, volunteers picked them and took them to a food bank at a local school. Every day, all summer long, families came to the school and took home fresh food.

## More Than Just Food

But the gardeners planted more than vegetables. They also grew flowers that they gave away with the vegetables. The gardeners worked hard not only to help feed the families, but also to give them something beautiful to enjoy.

❓ **How did the parishioners show care for God's creation?**

# Reach Out!

## Kinds of Care

In the space below, make a list of things that are necessary for God's creation to grow.

What does a **plant** need to grow healthy and strong?

_____

_____

_____

What does a **person** need to grow healthy and strong?

_____

_____

_____

Compare the lists. Which items are the same?

_____

_____

_____

## Make a Difference

**Share Creation**   Your class can follow the example of the St. Francis gardeners by growing something and sharing it with others. You can grow beautiful blooming plants and then take the flowers to a hospital, a senior care center, or another place where people will enjoy them.

73

**Ⓐ Work with Words**   Use the clues to solve the puzzle. Write the answer to each clue in the boxes. When you have finished, read down the column with the circles to find the hidden word.

1. What we call the first people's choice to disobey God

2. The summary of laws that God gave Moses

3. Said "yes" to God's will and became the Mother of Jesus

4. What Adam and Eve ate

5. God's loving care for all things; his will and plan for creation

6. How God tells humans about himself and makes his plan known

7. Steadfast and loyal in your commitment to God

8. What Joseph did after his brothers pleaded for Benjamin to be spared

9. A sacred promise or agreement between God and humans

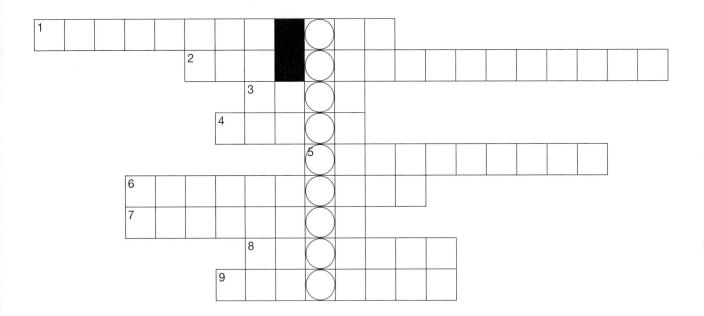

10. Hidden Word: _____ is another name for the Bible, or the word of God written in human words.

**B** **Check Understanding** Complete each sentence with the correct word from the Word Bank.

**WORD BANK**

plan
pharaoh's
journey
Moses
jealous

11. God asked Abram and Sarai to go on a long

_____ and live in a new land

called Canaan.

12. God has a _____ for all of his people.

13. Joseph's brothers sold him into slavery because

they were _____.

14. God gave the Ten Commandments to _____ to share

with his people.

15. As a baby, Moses was left in a basket by the Nile River, where he

was found by the _____ daughter.

**C** **Make Connections** Write a response to each question or statement.

16. Why is it important for you, like Jonah, to find a quiet place to pray?

_____

_____

17. What is the lesson of the story of Abraham and Sarah's waiting many

years to have a child?

_____

_____

Use all of the terms below to explain how you keep the third commandment.

Sunday                 worship                 rest

18.–20. _____

_____

_____

_____

_____

_____

# Unit 2
# Trinity

## In this unit you will...

learn that you are made in God's image and likeness and are to live and love in community. Showing love to others is a way we reflect the love of the Holy Trinity. Sin is the failure to do so. You will learn that Persons of the Trinity help you to do good and avoid evil. You do this by using your free will and following your conscience.

## Faith in Action!

**Catholic Social Teaching Principle:
Life and Dignity of the Human Person**

# Chapter 4 In God's Image

## Let Us Pray

**Leader:** God, we give you praise and thanks for all creation.
"When you send forth your breath, they are created,
and you renew the face of the earth."

*Psalm 104:30*

**All:** God, we give you praise and thanks for all creation. Amen.

**Activity**  **Let's Begin**

### Me I Am

There is no other ME I AM
who thinks the thoughts I do;
the world contains one ME I AM,
there is no room for two.
I am the only ME I AM
this earth shall ever see;
that ME I AM I always am
is no one else but ME!

A selection from the poem by Jack Prelutsky

Think about the best thing about being you.

• What special gifts and talents has God given you?

_____

_____

• **Design Your Coat of Arms** Design a coat of arms with symbols that tell what is special about you.

77

# An Image of Love

 **Focus** What does it mean to be created in the image of God?

God has given you life. He has created you and all people to reflect his own image of love. God's image can shine in you and in every person you meet. The story of Rosa Parks teaches us that all people should be treated equally.

## Faith Fact

James Augustine Healy was the first African American Catholic bishop in the United States. He was named bishop of Portland, Maine, in 1875.

A BIOGRAPHY

## Rosa Parks

On the evening of December 1, 1955, Rosa Parks boarded a public bus in Montgomery, Alabama, and took a seat in the *white section*. The bus filled quickly, and soon there were no more seats. The driver noticed that Rosa, a black woman, was not sitting in the *colored section*. He asked Rosa to move to the back of the bus, but she refused. She did not argue. She simply did not move.

Before the 1960s, African Americans were unjustly treated because of their skin color. They were separated from the rest of society in many ways. Long after that day on the bus, Rosa Parks wrote, "Our mistreatment was just not right, and I was tired of it. I kept thinking about my mother and my grandparents, and how strong they were. I knew there was a possibility of being mistreated, but an opportunity was being given to me to do what I had asked of others."

❓ **When have you observed that someone was being treated in a certain way simply because of the color of his or her skin?**

# Created with Dignity

Rosa Parks was a true hero of the struggle for human rights in the United States. Yet she began by doing one simple thing on a day when she was tired. Rosa expressed the very basic Christian belief that all people have **dignity** because they are created in God's image.

## ✝ SCRIPTURE

God created man in his image;
  in the divine image he created him;
  male and female he created them.

*Genesis 1:27*

God made you with a human body, and you have a **soul** that will live forever. God gave you the ability to think, to love, and to make choices. You can make choices for human dignity every day.

## Words of Faith

**Dignity** is self-worth. Every human is worthy of respect because he or she is made in the image of God.

**Soul** is the spiritual part of a human that lives forever.

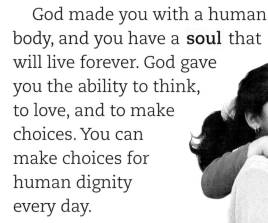

## Activity Share Your Faith

**Reflect:** Think of a time when you or someone you know showed respect or treated someone with dignity.

**Share:** Tell a partner what happened.

**Act:** List some ways you can protect the dignity of others.

_____

_____

_____

# Made to Love

 **Focus** What is sin?

God created you to be united to him and to all people. Every time you act in a loving way, you deepen your connection to God and to the members of the Church, the Body of Christ. When you choose to treat someone badly, you hurt this person and the whole community of faith. You choose not to show love and respect.

## Failure to Love

**Sin** is always a failure to love. A sinful thought, word, or act also hurts your friendship with God. Sin affects you, too, and keeps you from becoming the person God wants you to be.

There are two kinds of personal sin—mortal and venial. Serious sins, such as murder, are called mortal sins. They destroy the friendship a person has with God and with others. In order for a sin to be mortal, the act must be seriously wrong, you must know that it is seriously wrong, and you must freely choose to do it anyway.

Venial sins are less serious sins. They are things that you do, such as disobeying, cheating, and lying, or bad habits that you develop, such as being lazy or dishonest. Sometimes sin is a failure to act. This is a sin of omission. An example of this would be to remain silent when someone tells a joke that makes fun of another person or group. Venial sin hurts your friendship with God and others, but it does not destroy it.

## Love and Respect

**Social sin** refers to the results of sin that can build up over time in a community or nation. One example of social sin is not allowing someone of a certain race or group to buy a house in a certain neighborhood. Rosa Parks acted against inequality and social sin. She defended her own dignity and the dignity of others.

All people are equal. Every person has dignity and is worthy of respect because he or she is made in God's image. Because he is the Son of God, Jesus is the perfect image of God. You are called to become more like Jesus and to reflect the love and care that he shows all people.

## Words of Faith

**Sin** is a deliberate thought, word, deed, or omission contrary to the law of God.

**Social sin** is a sinful social structure or institution that builds up over time so that it affects the whole society.

## Activity    Connect Your Faith

**Ask for Forgiveness** Everybody sins, but not everybody asks for God's forgiveness. Write a personal prayer, asking God's forgiveness for some of your past actions.

# Seeing God's Image

**◉ Focus** Where do you see God's Image?

God shows you something of what he is like through his image in people and the reflections of him in the world he created. If you are alert to these clues, you will learn many things about him.

## Nature Shows the Glory of God

The loveliness of a flower or the brilliance of a sunset tells you something about God. Reflections of his glory may bring with them feelings of love or peace that fill your soul. Take a moment to look closely at nature and find the reflection of God in it.

## People Show the Glory of God

Think about people who have shown you love. These might include your parents or guardians, a good and loyal friend, an understanding teacher, or a devoted grandparent. A tiny baby may make you think of God's power and wonder. An older person may remind you of God's wisdom.

**❓ When have you seen a reflection of God in another person?**

# Live Your Faith

**Make a Collage**   By using pictures cut from magazines or by drawing the pictures yourself, make a collage of items that show reflections of God. These can include people, nature scenes, or other items. After you have finished, choose one item from your collage. Explain why it is special to you, and share your writing with the class.

My Special Item

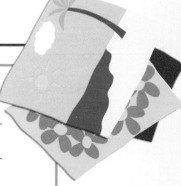

_____

_____

_____

# Prayer for Dignity and Respect

 Let Us Pray

*Gather and begin with the Sign of the Cross.*

*Sing together.*

Behold, behold, I make all things new, beginning
with you and starting from today.
Behold, behold, I make all things new, my promise
is true, for I am Christ the way.

"Behold, I Make All Things New" © 1994, The Iona Community,
GIA Publications, Inc., agent

Reader: God of life,

All: **We pray for
the dignity of life.**

Reader: God of creation,

All: **We pray for the
dignity of life.**

Reader: God, the source of all life,

All: **We pray for the dignity
of life.**

Reader: God, the protector of
all humanity,

All: **We pray for the dignity
of life.**

Leader: God, we give you praise
and thanks for all creation.

All: **Amen.**

**A** **Work with Words**   Circle True if a statement is true, and circle False if a statement is false. Correct any false statements.

1. A bully can never reflect God's image.

   True      False   _____

2. God is with everyone at all times in all places.

   True      False   _____

3. You commit a mortal sin when you cheat on a spelling test.

   True      False   _____

4. Rosa Parks was a victim of social sin.

   True      False   _____

5. Each person is unique and created by God.

   True      False   _____

**B** **Check Understanding**   Complete the following statements.

6. The _____ is the spiritual part of you that lives forever.

7. You have _____ because you are made in the image of God.

8. When you commit a _____, you hurt your friendship with God.

9. _____ and _____ show the glory of God.

10. You are _____ to show God's love and care to others, as Jesus did.

# Family Faith

## Catholics Believe

- Every person is worthy of respect because he or she is created in God's image.
- Each person has a soul that will live forever.

### SCRIPTURE

Read *Leviticus 19:1–18, 31–37* to learn other ways in which you can respect others and yourself and treat each person with dignity.

**GO online** www.osvcurriculum.com
For weekly scripture readings and seasonal resources

## Activity

# Live Your Faith

**Inside and Outside** When we respect our own dignity and that of others, we give honor to God, who has created us in his image. Gather some paper bags and magazines. Find pictures that show how you think others see you. Glue the pictures on the outside of a bag. Then find and place pictures inside the bag that show what God sees in you. Invite each person to share the contents of the bag if he or she wishes.

# People of Faith

**Saint Teresa Benedicta** was a teacher, a convert, and a Carmelite nun. Born Edith Stein, she lived during the first part of the twentieth century and took the name Teresa Benedicta. Her life was dedicated to teaching, especially the teaching of young girls and women. During the Nazi persecution of Jews, Edith was arrested and executed at Auschwitz. She is a model of the importance of forgiveness and reconciliation during a time of great violence. Saint Teresa's feast day is August 9.

▲ Saint Teresa Benedicta 1891–1942

## Family Prayer

Saint Teresa, may your life be a model. Pray for us that we might learn to forgive, even our enemies. Amen.

*In Unit 2 your child is learning about the TRINITY.*

**86** CCC *See Catechism of the Catholic Church 355–357, 362–366 for further reading on chapter content.*

# Chapter 5 Created for One Another

 **Let Us Pray**

**Leader:** Our Creator, we thank you for all the gifts we share.

"The earth is the Lord's and all it holds,
the world and those who live there."

*Psalm 24:1*

**All:** Our Creator, we thank you for all the gifts we share.
Amen.

## Activity

## Let's Begin

### The Chain of Life

The human race is a kind of chain
That binds the world as one.
We share the earth below our feet
And live beneath the sun.
Bodies, faces, voices, hands—
We each are given these.
All humans share the gift of life
And share a hope for peace.

Who are three links in your chain of life?

• Name one group to which you belong, and its purpose.

_____

_____

**Sketch Your "Environment"** Make a "community web" to show how people in your community depend on one another.

# Created to Love

 **Focus** What does love of neighbor have to do with love of God?

From the time of the first humans, people have formed groups. God's plan is for people to live together in love. This story shows how God wants people to live.

## A STORY

# HOLY GROUND

One night King Solomon noticed a man carrying sacks of wheat from one barn to another. "He must be a thief," Solomon thought. Soon a different man appeared, carrying sacks of wheat back to the original barn!

The next day Solomon called each man before him separately. To the first he said, "Why do you steal from your neighbor in the middle of the night?"

"I do not steal," the man said. "My neighbor is also my brother. He has a wife and children to feed, but he won't take any extra money from me. So every night I secretly carry wheat from my barn to his."

Solomon asked the second man the same question. The man answered, "I have a big family to help me, but my brother has to pay for help, and so he needs more wheat. He won't take it from me, so at night I secretly give the wheat to him."

Solomon said, "The holiest ground in Israel is here, where brothers love each other this much. I shall build a temple here."

From a Jewish teaching story

❓ **Why would a place where people share be a good spot for a temple?**

# Community of Love

The two brothers in the story tried to provide for each other's needs. Solomon called their land holy because he knew that God is present whenever people show their love for one another. The brothers had formed a **community** of love.

❓ **What are some other practical ways that members of a community show their love for one another?**

## Words of Faith

A **community** is a group of people who hold certain beliefs, hopes, and goals in common.

## The Common Good

You learned in the last chapter that God made all people in his image. You are more clearly an image of God when you reflect the love of the Holy Trinity to others.

**People who live in true communities work for the common good by**

- respecting the dignity of each person and acknowledging each person's right to freedom and self-expression, as long as others are not hurt.

- making sure that every person has a way to get the things that are necessary for life, such as food, shelter, and clothing.

- providing peace, security, and order in the community.

## Activity — Share Your Faith

**Reflect:** How do people in your neighborhood work for the common good?

**Share:** Tell the class about one of these activities.

**Act:** Draw something that represents this activity. Add your drawing to those of others in the class to make a collage.

# Christian Living

**◎ Focus** What does it mean to live a moral life?

Each person has individual rights that are balanced with a responsibility to respect and protect the rights of others. No one has unlimited freedom or an unlimited right to the earth's goods. When everyone's rights are in balance, the kingdom of God is close at hand.

You can see a good example of this in the story of the early Christians. From this passage we learn how they lived in the years just after the Resurrection and Ascension of Jesus.

## ✝ SCRIPTURE                                                      Acts 2:42–45

# The Communal Life

St. Lawrence Giving the Treasure of the Church to the Poor
by Bernardo Strozzi

They devoted themselves to the teaching of the apostles and to the communal life, to the breaking of the bread and to the prayers. Awe came upon everyone, and many wonders and signs were done through the apostles. All who believed were together and had all things in common; they would sell their property and possessions and divide them among all according to each one's need.

Acts 2:42–45

❓ **What examples can you give of people today who live as early Christians did?**

90

## Love One Another

The early Christians formed a community based on a common faith in Jesus Christ and his message. Their faith and love are an example for you today. Faith is your "yes" to all that God has revealed. God created all men and women equal and in his image. So respect for the rights and needs of others is part of faith.

Just as you cannot live in isolation from others, so you cannot believe alone. You believe as part of a larger community of faith. As a Christian believer, you are called to live a good moral life.

## Moral Living

The Christian moral life is a way of living in right relationship with God, yourself, and others. Christian **morality** includes following the Ten Commandments, the teachings of Jesus, and the teachings of the Church. It also includes following the good and just laws that work for the common good.

Christian families and your **parish** community are places where you can learn to live the Christian moral life.

## Activity  Connect Your Faith

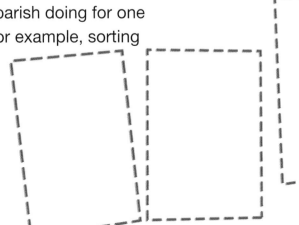

✐ **Service Charades**  Choose three activities you have noticed members of your parish doing for one another that show God's love (for example, sorting clothes for a rummage sale or ushering for Mass). Write the activities on three separate slips of paper. Place the papers in a container. Follow your teacher's direction.

# Living in Community

**Focus** How should you live as part of a community?

Your actions affect the lives of others. As part of the community of God's family, you have a responsibility to those around you. When you act responsibly, you help create a more loving community.

Here are some guidelines for becoming a good member of the community.

**Know** and **live** the Ten Commandments.

**Forgive** those who hurt you, and become a **peacemaker** when there is arguing and fighting.

Be **generous** to those who have less than you do. **Share** what you can of your time, talents, and possessions.

**Respect** everyone, especially those who are different from you.

**Help** those in need—people who are housebound, sick, lonely, afraid, very young, or very old.

❓ **How can you be a better member of your family, school, and parish community?**

# Live Your Faith

**Think About Your Community** For each of the letters in the word *community*, write a word or phrase that is important for a community. O is done for you.

**C** _____

**O** _____Opinions of others—respect them._____

**M** _____

**M** _____

**U** _____

**N** _____

**I** _____

**T** _____

**Y** _____

# Prebyer for Community

 Let Us Pray

*Gather and begin with the Sign of the Cross.*

*Sing together the refrain.*

Love one another. Love one another,
    as I have loved you.
Care for each other. Care for each other,
    as I care for you.

**Reader 1:** In this chain of life, we pray for our community.

**All:** **May we always respect one another.**

*Sing refrain.*

**Reader 2:** In the chain of this parish community, we pray for greater peace, security, and order.

**All:** **May we always respect one another.**

*Sing refrain.*

**Reader 3:** In the chain of our community gathered here, we pray for a right relationship with God, others, and ourselves.

**All:** **May we always respect one another.**

*Sing refrain.*

**Leader:** Let us pray.

*Bow your heads as the leader prays.*

**All:** **Amen.**

# Review

## A Work with Words

Solve the crossword puzzle.

### Down

1. A group of people with similar beliefs, working together toward a common goal

2. Living in right relationship with God, self, and others

4. Members of a community _____ on one another.

### Across

3. The result of respecting and working for everyone's rights in a community

5. When we show this to others, we follow God's way and live a moral life.

## B Check Understanding   Circle the word that best completes each statement.

6. In the story, King Solomon was (upset/pleased) with the love the two brothers showed.

7. Your individual rights are (balanced/unconnected) with your responsibility to respect and protect the rights of others.

8. God created (some/all) men and women equal and in his image.

9. A Catholic community where you can worship and learn is called a (parish/city).

10. As a Christian believer, you are called to live a (good/partly) moral life.

# Family Faith

## Catholics Believe

- God created people for one another, and all must work for the common good. Such love of neighbor reflects the love of the Holy Trinity.

- No one can believe alone, just as no one can live alone.

### ✝ SCRIPTURE

Read the Third Letter of John for advice about how a Christian community should receive strangers.

**GO online** www.osvcurriculum.com
For weekly scripture readings and seasonal resources

## Activity

# Live Your Faith

**Christian Actions** Read the passage about the communal life from *Acts 2:42–47*. Talk with your family about ways you could share with others as the early Christians did. List your ideas, and choose just one. After doing the action, talk about the experience. Discuss how each family member contributed to the good of others.

# People of Faith

Once a soldier and a bookseller, **John of God** gave his life to providing for those who were poor, homeless, or sick in body or mind. He set himself to doing things to help those in need, such as providing them with food and renting a house to give them shelter. This was the beginning of the order of the Brothers of Saint John of God. Saint John's love and care for those in need continues today. The brothers provide hospitality and care for those who are poor. Saint John's feast day is March 8.

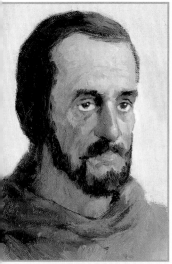
▲ Saint John of God
1495–1550

##  Family Prayer

Saint John, pray for us that we may find the wisdom to see people in need, even when the needs are not obvious. Guide us to be generous in giving gifts, time, and possessions for the good of others. Amen.

*In Unit 2 your child is learning about the TRINITY.*

**CCC** *See Catechism of the Catholic Church 1905–1912 for further reading on chapter content.*

# Chapter 6 Making Good Choices

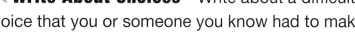

### Let Us Pray

**Leader:** God, give me the wisdom to make good choices.

"Teach me wisdom and knowledge,
for in your commands I trust."

*Psalm 119:66*

**All:** God, give me the wisdom to make good choices. Amen.

## Activity Let's Begin

● **Think About Choices**   When you were younger, your parents made most of your choices. Now that you are older, you are able to make more choices for yourself.

• What kinds of choices does your family allow you to make?

• What is an important choice that you have made?

Now think about how you make choices.
List two things that help you choose.

_____

_____

List two things that make choices harder.

_____

_____

✎ **Write About Choices**   Write about a difficult choice that you or someone you know had to make.

97

# Choices and Consequences

 **Focus** What is the proper use of free will?

You have the freedom to make choices, but all choices have consequences. In this story, Julia learns a lesson from a choice she makes.

A STORY

## Julia Decides

"Come on, Julia!" said Monica. "I really want to see the new movie at the Crosstown Cinema. I thought you wanted to see it, too."

"I do want to see it," Julia replied. "Maybe we can see it next week. My coach just called an extra soccer practice for this afternoon. I have to go."

"Well, you can go to soccer practice if you want to," said Monica. "I am going to the movie."

After Monica left, Julia got ready for practice. "I can see that movie later with my sister Lila," she thought as she tied her shoes. "Right now I have to work on my goal tending. The team is counting on me."

When Julia finally saw the movie, she enjoyed it. However, not as much as she enjoyed winning the award for most improved player at the end of the season!

❓ **What is something that happened because of Julia's choice?**

## Created with Free Will

Julia's story shows that all choices have consequences. You are responsible for your choices, too.

When God created you in his image, he gave you **free will**. With your free will, you make choices. Sometimes your choices are between right and wrong. Sometimes, as in Julia's case, they are between better and best. Whenever you make a good choice, you use God's gift of free will properly and you grow closer to God.

## A Helping Hand

God gives you many gifts to help you make good choices. God's most important gift is grace, which is the power of his own life within you. You received grace in a special way in the Sacrament of Baptism. You grow in God's grace through the Sacraments, prayer, and good moral choices.

In addition to his grace, God gives you the Ten Commandments and the Church to help you. God is always helping you develop a more loving relationship with him.

### Words of Faith

**Free will** is the God-given ability to choose between good and evil.

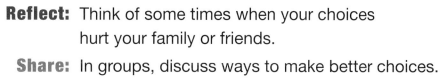

### Activity — Share Your Faith

**Reflect:** Think of some times when your choices hurt your family or friends.

**Share:** In groups, discuss ways to make better choices.

**Act:** Imagine the next chapter in the story of Julia and Monica's friendship. Role-play what you think might happen.

# Choosing to Love

**Focus** What is a strong conscience?

Good choices help you grow as a moral person. They build good habits and strengthen your relationship with God and others. Jesus calls us to act in ways that show love, even toward people whom we do not know. One day Jesus told this story to a scholar of the law.

## ✝ SCRIPTURE — Luke 10:30–37

# The Good Samaritan

Jesus said, "A Jewish traveler going from Jerusalem to Jericho was attacked by robbers who beat, robbed, and left him on the side of the road.

"A priest saw the injured traveler and moved to the other side of the road. Later a Jewish leader came to the same place, and when he saw the traveler, he too moved to the other side of the road. Finally, a Samaritan came to the place where the traveler lay dying. Unlike the others, the Samaritan stopped. He treated and bandaged the traveler's wounds. He carried him on his own animal to an inn, where he cared for him. The next day, when the Samaritan was leaving, he gave the innkeeper money and told him, 'Take care of this man. If you spend more than what I have given you, I will repay you when I return.'"

Based on *Luke 10:30–37*

❓ **What was difficult about the choice the Samaritan made?**

❓ **When is it difficult for you to make good choices?**

# God's Gift of Conscience

Good choices strengthen your relationship with God and others. Sin weakens or destroys that relationship. Sin is always a failure to love God and others. When you use your free will to sin, you always become less free.

You probably know when you have done something wrong, even if no one has seen you. The "inner voice" that tells you so is your **conscience**. Conscience is your free will and your reason working together. They direct you to choose what is good and avoid what is wrong.

You have the seeds of a strong conscience within you. It is your job to strengthen, or form, your own conscience. You cannot do this alone.

## Words of Faith

**Conscience** is the gift from God that helps you know the difference between right and wrong and helps you choose what is right.

## FORMING YOUR CONSCIENCE

| | |
|---|---|
| The Holy Spirit ⟷ | *Strengthens you to make good choices* |
| Prayer and study ⟷ | *Help you think things through* |
| Scripture and Church teaching ⟷ | *Guide your decisions* |
| Parents, teachers, and wise people ⟷ | *Give you good advice* |

## Activity — Connect Your Faith

Dear Pam,

I'm invited to sleep over at my friend's house on Friday night. She has a video for us to watch. My parents already told me this video is not for children. I'm a little worried, but my friend said, "Don't be such a baby. They will never know." What should I do?

Confused

**"Dear Pam"** Imagine that you write an advice column in a newspaper. What advice would you give to help the letter-writer use God's gift of conscience?

_____

_____

_____

_____

_____

_____

# Step by Step

 **Focus** How do you make decisions?

Making good moral decisions takes practice. Remember the words *stop*, *think*, *pray*, and *choose*. They are steps to help you make decisions. These words will remind you what to do when you are faced with a moral choice.

## **S**top

**Take your time** Do not make a snap decision or act on your first idea.
- Important choices can affect you, others, and your relationship with God.
- Give yourself time, and you are more likely to make a good decision.

## **T**hink

**Consider your choices** Think about what might happen if you make each choice.
- Say a prayer to the Holy Spirit for guidance.
- Listen to your conscience.
- Consider what the Bible and the Church teach you.
- Consult with your family and teachers.

## **P**ray

**Ask for help in choosing** Reflect on what God is calling you to do.
- Pray again for help and guidance from the Holy Spirit.
- Ask for wisdom and courage to make the best choice.

## **C**hoose

**Make up your mind** Decide what you will do.
- Be confident that if you think and pray about your decision, you will make the right choice.
- Act on your choice.

These four steps may not help you make the easiest choice or the most popular choice, but they will help you make the best choice.

# Live Your Faith

**Ask "What If?"** Think about what you might do in the situations described below. Share your ideas with your class.

**you** had $100 to spend?

**you** wanted to change something about yourself?

**your** best friend let you down?

# WHAT iF...

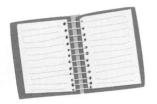

**you** forgot to do your homework?

**you** knew that a friend of yours was doing something dangerous?

Use the following questions to reflect on your discussion.

Did you use the steps to help you decide? For which choices were the steps helpful? Who else made the same choices that you did? Was someone else's choice better than yours?

**Write** Tell three things that you learned from this activity.

1. _____

_____

2. _____

_____

3. _____

_____

# Prayer of Reflection

 Let Us Pray

*Gather and begin with the Sign of the Cross.*

**Leader:** In prayer, you listen for God's voice to guide you. Close your eyes and think about a time when you were afraid and didn't know what to do. Listen to this story about a man named Elijah, who heard God's voice in a very surprising way when he was afraid.

**Reader:** *Read 1 Kings 19:9–14.*

**Leader:** Sit quietly and notice whether you can hear God whispering to you inside your heart. What is God saying to you? What do you want to say to God?

**Leader:** God of the whispering sound, help us be still and listen for your voice to guide us.

**All:** **Amen.**

*Sing together.*

For you, O Lord, my soul in stillness waits, truly my hope is in you.

"My Soul in Stillness Waits" © 1982, GIA Publications, Inc.

**A Work with Words**   Complete each sentence with the correct term from the Word Bank.

**WORD BANK**

moral
free will
conscience
God
grace

1. When God created you in his image, he gave you

   _____ to use in making good choices.

2. Your _____ is the gift from God that helps you know the difference between right and wrong.

3. Good choices help you grow as a

   _____ person.

4. Sin weakens or destroys your relationship with

   _____ and with others.

5. God's life in you is _____.

**B Make Connections**   Write responses on the lines below.

6. What is the lesson of the story of the Good Samaritan?

   _____

   _____

7. How do prayer and study help you?

   _____

   _____

8. What can help you make good decisions?

   _____

   _____

9. What happens when you choose to sin?

   _____

   _____

10. To whom can you go when you need advice?

    _____

    _____

# Family Faith

## Catholics Believe

- God has given you free will so that you can make good choices.

- Your conscience is the "inner voice" that helps you choose what is good.

### ✝ SCRIPTURE

*Matthew 26:69–75* is about a choice Peter made the night before Jesus died. Read the story together, and talk about the lesson it teaches.

**GO online** **www.osvcurriculum.com**
For weekly scripture readings and seasonal resources

## Activity

# Live Your Faith

**Read Together** Read through the newspaper to find articles about people who have made good or bad moral choices. As a family, discuss how conscience guides people to make better moral decisions.

# People of Faith

**Charles Lwanga** was a young servant in the king's court in Uganda. The king hated Christians. He commanded his servants to join in immoral activities. Charles, the master of the court pages, and twenty-one other young Christians refused. They were killed in 1886 for following their consciences. They prayed while they were dying. Saint Charles Lwanga and his companions are known as the African Martyrs. Their feast day is June 3.

▲ Saint Charles Lwanga and his companions

##  Family Prayer

Saint Charles, pray for us that we may follow our consciences, even when it is hard to do so. Help us learn from you the meaning of freedom. Amen.

# Faith in Action!
## CATHOLIC SOCIAL TEACHING

In this unit you learned that God created humans in his own image. This means that all people have dignity and are worthy of respect. It is your responsibility to respect the dignity of all people.

## Life and Dignity

All humans have a special place in God's plan. As followers of Jesus, you have an important duty to help one another use God's gifts to live as he has called you to live.

God wants all people to have the food, water, and shelter they need to live happy and healthy lives. He also wants you to treat all people with respect. Part of showing respect for people is asking them what they need and then helping them to help themselves.

❓ **What are some ways you can show respect for human life and dignity?**

# A Tale of Two Parishes

When the people of a parish in America wanted to help a parish overseas, they learned about dignity and respect.

The people of St. George's Parish in New York heard about a parish in Coq Chante (KOHK•SHAHNT), Haiti, named St. Michael the Archangel. They learned that the people there have poor living conditions and suffer from health problems. So some parishioners went to Haiti with supplies, money, and gifts. They gave these things to the Haitians.

The people of St. George's soon realized that they were not helping the Haitians build a future. Before the Americans could help, they had to learn what the people of Coq Chante needed most.

## A Better Way

St. George's parishioners decided to join the Haiti Parish Twinning Program of the Americas. In this program a Haitian parish with certain needs is matched with a parish in America that can help. St. George's parishioners learned that the people of Coq Chante desperately needed medical care. Now, once a year, St. George's sends doctors, nurses, and other volunteers to care for hundreds of people in Coq Chante. Volunteers are also helping build a school and a clinic. Giving the Haitians what they need most is a way of helping that shows respect.

❓ How does the Haiti Parish Twinning Program show respect for people's lives and dignity?

108

# Reach Out!

## Reflect

The Twinning Program sends help to people such as the residents of Coq Chante, Haiti. In addition to medical care, what other types of aid might the villagers need?

_____

_____

How would these types of aid improve the people's lives?

_____

_____

How would these types of aid respect the people's dignity?

_____

_____

The Twinning Program is not just about helping people who are poor. The people from St. George's Parish learned a valuable lesson. What was it?

_____

_____

_____

How might this lesson help St. George's parishioners be better followers of Jesus?

_____

_____

_____

## Make a Difference

**Write a Skit**   Now it is your turn. Together with your classmates, use what you have learned to write and present a skit about children in Haiti and in the United States. Close your performance with a prayer that asks for help in respecting human life and dignity.

**A** **Work with Words** Write the correct word after each definition. Then find the word in the word search. Some words may be written backwards.

| | | | | | | | | | |
|---|---|---|---|---|---|---|---|---|---|
| E | C | N | E | I | C | S | N | O | C |
| F | C | D | E | V | Q | T | Y | Y | L |
| O | L | N | N | P | I | U | H | T | G |
| C | M | J | E | K | E | P | S | I | R |
| I | L | M | L | I | X | U | X | N | A |
| W | D | I | G | N | I | T | Y | U | C |
| J | D | Y | P | P | V | S | K | M | E |
| C | R | E | A | T | E | I | N | M | Y |
| N | J | E | Z | Q | M | U | S | O | A |
| X | V | Z | O | O | R | E | S | C | C |

1. God's own life within you _____

2. To make something from nothing _____

3. The inner voice that helps you know right from wrong

   _____

4. A group of people with common beliefs and goals

   _____

5. A person's self-worth and respect _____

**B** **Check Understanding** Match each description in Column 1 with the correct term in Column 2. Terms may be used more than once.

**Column 1**

_____ 6. Cheating on homework

_____ 7. Staying silent while someone is being teased

_____ 8. Lying to a friend

_____ 9. Choosing friends by the color of their skin

_____ 10. Murder

**Column 2**

a. mortal sin

b. venial sin

c. sin of omission

d. social sin

Match each description in Column 1 with the correct term in Column 2.

**Column 1**

_____ **11.** the spiritual part of a human that lives forever

_____ **12.** a deliberate thought, word, deed, or omission contrary to the law of God

_____ **13.** a Catholic community with shared spiritual beliefs and worship

_____ **14.** living in right relationship with God, yourself, and others

_____ **15.** the ability God has given you to make good choices

**Column 2**

**a.** sin

**b.** free will

**c.** morality

**d.** parish

**e.** soul

**Ⓒ** **Make Connections**   Write responses on the lines below.

**16.** What is the difference between mortal sin and venial sin?

_____

_____

**17.** How does social sin affect communities?

_____

_____

**18.** How can you work for the common good?

_____

_____

**19.** How would you describe morality?

_____

_____

**20.** What can you do to respect the dignity of others?

_____

_____

# Unit 3
# Jesus Christ

## In this unit you will...

learn that Jesus wants people to be happy and to carry his message of the goodness of God's kingdom into the world. He shared that message in his teachings, most especially the Beatitudes. Jesus calls us to trust in the Father and to be a blessing to others by living the Great Commandment of love. Jesus teaches us to praise God with worship, by honoring his name, and by keeping Sunday holy.

## Faith in Action!

**Catholic Social Teaching Principle: Rights and Responsibilities of the Human Person**

# Chapter 7 You Are Blessed!

## Let Us Pray

**Leader:** All glory to you, God almighty!

"Praise the LORD, who is so good;
God's love endures forever."

*Psalm 136:1*

**All:** All glory to you, God almighty! Amen.

## Activity

# Let's Begin

**Be Blessed** You may have heard someone say, "We are so blessed!" Some people think of prizes, gifts, or lots of money as blessings. Others think of good health, the love of family, or the joy of good times with friends.

Now think about what it means to be blessed.

• How do you share your blessings with others?

_____

_____

_____

**Count Your Blessings** Write about or draw five blessings in your life.

# True Happiness

 **Focus** What does it mean to be a blessing for others?

In this retelling of a famous story, happiness is spread by unlikely partners.

A STORY

# THE HAPPY PRINCE

High above the city, on a tall column, stood the statue of the Happy Prince. He was gilded all over with thin leaves of gold; for eyes he had two bright sapphires, and a large red ruby glowed in his sword-hilt.

One evening, a tiny swallow that was flying south stopped to rest in the statue's shadow. She looked up and saw tears coming from the prince's eyes.

"Why are you weeping?" the swallow asked. "I thought you were the Happy Prince!"

"When I was alive," answered the statue, "anything sad was hidden from me. But now I look down and see all of the city's pain.

"Look! There is a poor seamstress working on a beautiful gown for the queen. Her little boy has a fever. He would like oranges, but she has only river water to give him. Will you take her the ruby from my sword?" The swallow hesitated but then agreed.

"Just this once!" she said.

❓ **Why do you think the swallow agreed to stay and help the prince?**

# THE PRICE OF HAPPINESS

Each day, the prince convinced the swallow to stay on. Together, they gave away all the riches the prince had, including his sapphire eyes and the leaves of gold covering his garments.

When winter came, the swallow soon died from the cold. City leaders melted down the statue to make something else from it. But when they did, its heart would not burn! The prince's heart and the dead swallow ended up side by side in a trash heap.

God looked down one day from heaven and said to an angel, "Bring me the two most precious things in the city." The angel brought him the prince's heart and the dead bird.

"You have chosen well," said God, "for in my kingdom of heaven this little bird shall sing forevermore, and the Happy Prince shall praise me."

## Activity — Share Your Faith

**Reflect:** How does the Happy Prince know who needs help?

**Share:** By the end of the story, who is blessed? Discuss your response with a partner.

**Act:** Describe one way that you can be a blessing for others.

_____

_____

_____

# Jesus Brings God's Blessing

 **Focus** What did Jesus teach about the true meaning of happiness?

"The Happy Prince" tells who the writer believed would be blessed by God. In this Bible story, Jesus taught about who is blessed and how to be a blessing for others.

✝ **SCRIPTURE** Matthew 5:1–10

## The Sermon on the Mount

One day Jesus stood in the midst of his Apostles and a great crowd of followers. He taught them with these words:

"Blessed are the poor in spirit,
for theirs is the kingdom of heaven.

Blessed are they who mourn,
for they will be comforted.

Blessed are the meek,
for they will inherit the land.

Blessed are they who hunger and thirst
for righteousness,
for they will be satisfied.

Blessed are the merciful,
for they will be shown mercy.

Blessed are the clean of heart,
for they will see God.

Blessed are the peacemakers,
for they will be called children of God.

Blessed are they who are persecuted
for the sake of righteousness,
for theirs is the kingdom of heaven."

From *Matthew 5:1–10*

# The Beatitudes

The Church calls this teaching of Jesus the **Beatitudes**. The word *beatitude* means "blessing" or "happiness." The Beatitudes tell you how to be a blessing for others so that you, too, will be blessed by God. They are about the lasting happiness that God calls you to have. God desires all people to work for his kingdom and to share in eternal life with him.

The eight **Beatitudes** are teachings of Jesus that show the way to true happiness and tell the way to live in God's kingdom now and always.

Blessed are the poor in spirit . . .
Depend on God, not on material things.

Blessed are the meek . . .
Be gentle and humble with others.

Blessed are the merciful . . .
Forgive others and ask their forgiveness.

Blessed are the peacemakers . . .
Work to bring people together. Look for ways to solve problems peacefully.

Blessed are they who mourn . . .
Share other people's sorrows and joys.

Blessed are those who hunger and thirst for righteousness . . .
Help all people treat others justly, and help change unjust conditions.

Blessed are the clean of heart . . .
Be faithful to God and to God's ways.

Blessed are those who are persecuted for the sake of righteousness . . .
In difficult times, trust in God and stand up for what is right.

## Activity  Connect Your Faith

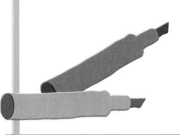

**A Blessing Scene**    On a separate sheet of paper, draw a picture of what you have done to live one of the Beatitudes.

# Pray for Others

 **Focus** How can you share blessings through prayer?

You live the Beatitudes by showing God's love and care to others. Another way to show that you care is to pray for others.

## Share Blessings

Intercession, or petition, is a kind of prayer in which you ask God for something for another person or for the community. It is a generous, thoughtful prayer, and it is one of the types of prayers that Jesus prayed for others.

Just before the presentation of the gifts at Mass, the whole assembly offers prayers of intercession to God. These prayers are often said for members of the church, religious and government leaders, and people in the news. Here are some examples of when you might want to say a prayer of intercession.

When a friend is very unhappy

When a friend has to make a hard decision

When you have heard on the news that people have lost their homes during a flood

When a family member is sick

When an adult has lost a job

When a member of your parish has had someone in his or her family die

❓ **For what other people would you say a prayer of intercession?**

# Live Your Faith

**Write Prayers for Others**   Write a prayer of intercession for each of the people in the situations below. Then think of two people in your life, and write a prayer of intercession for each of them in the spaces provided.

Jenny's mother was in a car accident. She has been in the hospital for a long time. Jenny is upset and very scared.

Kevin's parents have been fighting a lot lately. It makes him sad, and he worries that they might separate.

# Prayer of Blessing

 Let Us Pray

*Gather and begin with the Sign of the Cross.*

**Leader:** Brothers and sisters, praise God, who is rich in mercy.

**All:** **Blessed be God forever.**

**Reader 1:** *Read Philippians 4:4–7.*

**All:** **Blessed be God forever.**

**Reader 2:** Loving God, you created all the people of the world, and you know each of us by name.

**All:** **Blessed be God forever.**

**Reader 3:** We thank you for our lives. Bless us with your love and friendship.

**All:** **Blessed be God forever.**

**Reader 4:** May we grow in wisdom, knowledge, and grace.

**All:** **Blessed be God forever.**

**Leader:** May we be blessed in the name of the Father, the Son, and the Holy Spirit.

**All:** **Amen.**

*Sing together.*

For your gracious blessing,
for your wondrous word,

for your loving kindness,
we give thanks, O God.

"For Your Gracious Blessing" Traditional

WE
RECYCLE

**A** **Work with Words**   Complete the following paragraph with the correct words from the Word Bank.

**1.–5.** Jesus gave us the _____ to help us be a _____ for others. As we share our blessings with others, we help them find true _____. Through the _____ Beatitudes, Jesus tells us about being blessed by God and finding true happiness. People who will inherit the land are blessed as _____.

**B** **Check Understanding**   Fill in the circle next to the answer that best completes each statement.

**6.**   People who are poor in spirit are those who depend on _____.

⭘ material things   ⭘ God        ⭘ themselves

**7.**   God wants all people to share _____ with him.

⭘ eternal life     ⭘ beatitudes   ⭘ material things

**8.**   Working to bring people together is a way to be _____.

⭘ meek          ⭘ poor in spirit   ⭘ a peacemaker

**9.**   You can show care by _____.

⭘ praying for others   ⭘ taking from others   ⭘ being selfish

**10.**   Prayers of _____ ask God for something for another person or for a community.

⭘ righteousness   ⭘ intercession   ⭘ friendship

# Family Faith

## Catholics Believe

- The Beatitudes are eight teachings that describe the reign of God that Jesus announced when he lived on earth.

- The Beatitudes show you how to live and act as a follower of Jesus.

### SCRIPTURE

Read *Luke 6:20–26* to find out about the Beatitudes in the Gospel according to Luke.

**GO online** www.osvcurriculum.com
For weekly scripture readings and seasonal resources

## Activity

# Live Your Faith

**Blessing Chart** Work at being a blessing. Make a chart titled "A Blessing for Others" to display in your home. Write each family member's name below the title. Each time you notice someone in the family living one of the Beatitudes, draw a heart next to his or her name. You can also write a word next to the name to tell the goodness that person showed.

A Blessing for Others
Mom ♥ ♥ ♥
Dad ♥ ♥ ♥
Sister ♥
Brother ♥

# People of Faith

▲ Saint Martin de Porres
1575–1639

**Martin** was born in Lima, Peru. His father was Spanish, and his mother was a freed black slave from Panama. Martin became a Dominican brother and spent his life doing simple good works for those in need. He went throughout the city, caring for those who were sick and poor. He was a blessing to all he met, even animals. Because he was meek and pure of heart, he saw that the simplest work gave honor to God if it served others.

## Family Prayer

Saint Martin, help us do good for those in need. Give us strength to follow your example and live for others. Amen.

*In Unit 3 your child is learning about JESUS CHRIST.*

# Chapter 8 The Great Commandment

## Let Us Pray

**Leader:** Merciful God, help us know and do your will.

"LORD, teach me the way of your laws;
I shall observe them with care."

*Psalm 119:33*

**All:** Merciful God, help us know and do your will. Amen.

## Let's Begin

### Activity

● **Signs of Love**  Elena keeps a photo album. Some of the pictures are of times and places in which she showed God's love to others. Other pictures show ways that other people showed God's love to her.

If this were your album, what picture would you show of yourself?

• Name three ways you have shown God's love to others.

_____

_____

_____

**Write Your Thanks**  Write three thank-you notes to friends and family members to remind them of times when they have shown God's love to you.

My friends and I helped gather clothes for the needy.

# Following Jesus

 **Focus** How is the Great Commandment like the Ten Commandments?

Elena and her family follow Jesus by sharing their love with others. Once, Jesus asked a young man to show his love for others in a very generous way.

## ✝ SCRIPTURE                                      Matthew 19:16–22

# *The Rich Young Man*

One day when Jesus was teaching, a young man asked, "What must I do to live forever with God?"

Jesus answered, "Keep the commandments."

"Which commandments?" the young man asked. Jesus listed some of the Ten Commandments for him.

"I keep all those commandments!" the young man said happily. "What else do I need to do?"

"If you really wish to be perfect," Jesus said, "go and sell everything you have. Give the money to people who are poor. Then come and follow me."

The young man's smile faded, for he was very rich. He could not imagine giving everything away, so he went away sad.

*Based on Matthew 19:16–22*

Jesus asked the rich young man to make a very big sacrifice. He knew that the young man's love for his possessions could keep him from loving God completely. When Jesus tested the young man to see how important his possessions were, the young man could not part with them.

❓ **What possession would be the hardest for you to give away? Why?**

# The Great Commandment

Jesus taught that keeping the Ten Commandments includes more than checking off items on a list. Each commandment shows you a way to love God and love others with your whole heart and soul.

Words of Faith

The **Great Commandment** is the twofold command to love God above all and your neighbor as yourself.

## ✝ SCRIPTURE

"You shall love the Lord, your God, with all your heart, with all your soul, and with all your mind. This is the greatest and the first commandment. The second is like it: You shall love your neighbor as yourself. The whole law and the prophets depend on these two commandments."

Based on *Matthew 22:37–40*

Therefore, the **Great Commandment** sums up the Ten Commandments, the whole law, and what the prophets taught.

## Activity Share Your Faith

**Believe**

**Reflect:** Look at an advertisement in a magazine. Does this ad support the teaching of Jesus?

**Share:** Share your response with a partner.

**Act:** As a group, write an ad that supports the teaching of Jesus.

# Love in Action

 **Focus** How can you live the Great Commandment?

The command to love is not a weak or soft bit of advice, as this tale makes clear.

A FOLKTALE

## *The Paper Dragon*

Long ago, a Chinese artist named Mi Fei was asked by his people to defend them against Sui Jen, a dragon. "Who dares to disturb me?" roared the dragon.

"I am Mi Fei," whispered the artist. "Spare our people."

The dragon's red eyes glowed. "Before I will do that, Mi Fei, you must perform three tasks. What is the most important thing your people have discovered?"

"I think it is paper," exclaimed Mi Fei.

"Ridiculous!" snorted the dragon. "Bring me fire, then, wrapped in paper, or I will destroy you!" After much thought, Mi Fei brought the dragon a paper lantern with a candle glowing inside.

Next, the dragon asked Mi Fei to bring the wind captured by paper. Mi Fei brought a paper fan.

The dragon gave Mi Fei his third task. "Bring me the strongest thing in the world, carried in paper." Mi Fei thought and thought. Then he painted all the loving people of his village. He returned, showed his painting, and said, "Love can move mountains; love brings light and life."

Suddenly, Sui Jen began to shrink. "Mi Fei," he said, "truly, the strongest thing in the world is love." When Mi Fei looked down, he found a small paper dragon.

❓ **What is the message of this story?**

# Jesus Shows the Way

"The Paper Dragon" is only a folktale. However, it makes the very important point that the power of love can make a difference. God the Father sent his Son to show all people how to live in love as Mi Fei did. Jesus cared most for those who were poor, helpless, and suffering, and he calls all of his followers to do the same.

## Acts of Charity

With the strength of the Holy Spirit, whom Jesus sent, you have the power to reach out to others in love, just as Jesus did. The Holy Spirit breathed **charity** into you at your baptism.

Jesus' Great Commandment tells you to love others as you love yourself. Christians see the needs of others and help meet those needs. The Church has named seven acts of kindness that you can do to meet the physical needs of others. They are called the **Corporal Works of Mercy**.

## Words of Faith

**Charity** is the virtue of love. It directs people to love God above all things and their neighbor as themselves for the love of God.

The **Corporal Works of Mercy** are actions that meet the physical needs of others.

---

**Activity**

## Connect Your Faith

**Recognize Works of Mercy** Draw lines to match each Corporal Work of Mercy with an action. Then circle the actions that you have done.

| Works of Mercy | Actions |
| --- | --- |
| Clothe the naked. | Volunteer to help serve a meal at a shelter. |
| Shelter the homeless. | Attend a funeral. |
| Feed the hungry. | Donate clothes to those in need. |
| Give drink to the thirsty. | Donate books to a prison. |
| Visit the imprisoned. | Visit a homebound relative. |
| Visit the sick. | Donate money to a homeless shelter. |
| Bury the dead. | Set up a free lemonade stand on a hot summer day. |

# Care for Others

**Focus** How can you help people as Jesus did?

People all over the world are in need. Some of them are in your parish or neighborhood. If you pay attention, you may find that you know people who need your loving help.

## Many Kinds of Need

When you think of people in need, do you imagine people who are homeless, hungry, and sick? The Corporal Works of Mercy teach us that there are many kinds of need. It is not always easy to see what those needs are. Here are some people you might see who need your help.

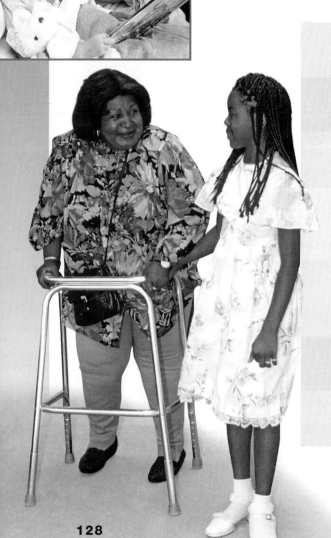

**Clothe the naked**
A child on the playground loses his sweater.

**Shelter the homeless**
A neighbor child forgets her house key.

**Feed the hungry**
A classmate drops his lunch tray.

**Give drink to the thirsty**
A teammate does not have a water bottle.

**Visit the imprisoned**
A neighbor lady has no way to get to the grocery store.

**Visit the sick**
Your cousin has a broken leg.

**Bury the dead**
The mother of one of your classmates dies.

❓ **How could you help each of these people in need?**

# Live Your Faith

**Spread the Word**   Write a newspaper article about someone you know who cares for and loves people in need. Explain **who** this person is, **what** the person did, and **what** happened next. In your article, compare this person's actions with what Jesus might have done in a similar situation. Draw a picture to go with the article. Don't forget to give the article a headline.

## Cool School News

Headline _____

_____

Story _____

_____

_____

_____

_____

_____

_____

_____

# Celebration of the Word

 **Let Us Pray**

*Gather and begin with the Sign of the Cross.*

Leader:  God of Mercy, we gather to remind ourselves of your love and mercy.

Reader 1:  A reading from the First Letter to the Corinthians.

*Read 1 Corinthians 13:2–7.*

The word of the Lord.

All:  **Thanks be to God.**

Reader 2:  Lord, give us the gift of patience.

All:  **We want to live in your love.**

Reader 3:  Lord, give us the gift of kindness.

All:  **We want to live in your love.**

Reader 4:  Lord, help us think of others.

All:  **We want to live in your love.**

Leader:  Let us pray.

*Bow your heads as the leader prays.*

All:  **Amen.**

*Sing together.*

*Ubi caritas et amor,*
*ubi caritas Deus ibi est.*
Live in charity and steadfast love,
live in charity;
God will dwell with you.

**A** **Work with Words**   Use the words in the Word Bank to write five of the Corporal Works of Mercy. Use the lines below.

| the | drink | dead | feed | shelter | bury |
| hungry | the | the | give | thirsty | homeless |
| sick | visit | to | the | the | |

1. _____

2. _____

3. _____

4. _____

5. _____

**B** **Check Understanding**   Circle True if a statement is true, and circle False if a statement is false. Correct each false statement.

6. The Corporal Works of Mercy make it hard for you to grow as a Christian.
   True      False   _____

7. Only adults have the ability to care for and help others.
   True      False   _____

8. The Great Commandment is a law of love.
   True      False   _____

9. The Great Commandment can be restated in this way: "First love God, and then love others as you love yourself."
   True      False   _____

10. The virtue of charity helps you perform the Corporal Works of Mercy.
    True      False   _____

# Family Faith

## Catholics Believe

- The Great Commandment is to love God with all your heart, strength, and mind and to love your neighbor as yourself.

- The Great Commandment sums up all of the teachings of the Ten Commandments.

### ✝ SCRIPTURE

Read *Isaiah 58:6–10* and *Matthew 25:34–40* to find the Corporal Works of Mercy in the Bible.

**GO online** www.osvcurriculum.com
For weekly scripture readings and seasonal resources

## Activity

# Live Your Faith

**Acts of Love** Design a greeting card, and make a special family food. Deliver both to someone who is sick, elderly, or a new parent or neighbor. Spend time visiting. On the way home, talk about the experience and how it felt to live the Great Commandment.

# People of Faith

▲ Saint Katharine
Drexel
1858–1955

**Katharine Drexel** devoted her money and her life to those who were poor. She did missionary work among African Americans and Native Americans. She founded the Sisters of the Blessed Sacrament to help educate members of these ethnic groups. Katharine also established many schools on Native American reservations and the first and only Catholic university for African Americans. Saint Katharine's feast day is March 3.

##  Family Prayer

Saint Katharine, pray for us that we may follow the way of Jesus. Help us live out the Corporal Works of Mercy in our daily lives. Amen.

*In Unit 3 your child is learning about JESUS CHRIST.*

# Chapter 9 Honoring God

## Let Us Pray

**Leader:** We praise and honor your holy name, O Lord.

"Then call on me in time of distress;
I will rescue you, and you shall honor me."

*Psalm 50:15*

**All:** We praise and honor your holy name, O Lord. Amen.

## Activity — Let's Begin

**A Place of Honor** "What are you building?" Jeremy asked. "A spice rack?"

"No," said Vernique. "It's something for the whole family. It's a place of honor."

Jeremy was doubtful. "What does that mean? It just looks like a shelf."

"It's a place to put things that make us proud of our family," Vernique replied. "It's for Dad's bowling trophy and my science fair certificate—and Mom's picture from when she shook hands with the mayor."

"Can I put the pottery bowl I made there, too?"

"Sure," said Vernique.

• What you would put in a place of honor for your family?

_____

• What would your family or friends add to the shelf?

_____

**Create a Poster of Honor** Make a poster of honor, using symbols for yourself, your family, and friends.

**133**

# God's People Forget

 **Focus** What does it mean to praise and honor God?

## Faith Fact

The ancient laws that God gave the Israelites through Moses are known as the Mosaic Law.

God created each person to be unique. God also created all humans to be alike in a most important way. He created everyone in his own image. Once, the Hebrew people forgot to show God the honor and respect that was due to the giver of such a gift.

✝ **S C R I P T U R E** Exodus 32:1–20

## The Golden Calf

**M**oses was with God on Mount Sinai for forty days and forty nights. When the people became aware of Moses' delay, they gathered around Aaron and said to him, "Come, make us a god who will be our leader; as for the man Moses who brought us out of the land of Egypt, we do not know what has happened to him." Aaron collected all their gold and melted it down to be formed into a golden calf. Then Aaron built an altar before the calf and declared a feast. The people brought sacrifices and worshipped the calf, saying: "This is your God, O Israel, who brought you out of the land of Egypt."

God then told Moses to return to the people and tell them how angry he was. Moses returned to the camp and destroyed the calf, turning it to powder.

*Based on Exodus 32:1–20*

❓ **Why do you think the people made the golden calf?**

❓ **Why was Moses upset?**

# Honoring God

The sin of God's people occurred while Moses was receiving the stone tablets of the Ten Commandments from God. The first commandment says, "I am the Lord your God. You shall not have strange gods before me."

The first commandment requires you to honor and worship only God. **Worship** is the adoration and praise that is due to God. You worship God when you celebrate Mass with your parish community, when you pray, and when you live a life that puts God first. Worshipping an object or a person instead of God, as the people worshipped the golden calf, is called **idolatry**.

When you worship God, you show your belief in him as the source of creation and salvation. You show that you, and all creatures, rely on him for life. You show your trust and hope in him. This is why fortune-telling or thinking that we can control nature and know the things that God knows are against the first commandment.

## Words of Faith

To **worship** God is to adore and praise God, especially in prayer and liturgy.

**Idolatry** is the sin of worshipping an object or a person instead of God. It is letting anything or anyone become more important than God.

❓ **What are some things that people sometimes place ahead of God?**

## Activity — Share Your Faith

**Reflect:** In what ways do you worship God?

**Share:** Share your responses with a partner.

**Act:** Choose the type of worship that means the most to you. Then write a few sentences explaining why this is your favorite way to worship.

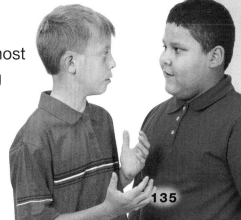

_____

_____

_____

135

# Respect for God

**Focus** What do the second and third commandments tell you to do?

The second commandment is connected to the first: "You shall not take the name of the Lord in vain." God's name is sacred, or holy, because God is sacred. When God called Moses to be the leader of his people, God revealed his name to Moses. God shared his name with his people because he loved and trusted them. In return, God's people are to bless and praise God's holy name.

This commandment calls you to always use the name of God with reverence and respect. Respecting God's name is a sign of the respect God deserves. It is a sin against God's name to curse or to use God's name to swear to a lie. To seriously dishonor the name of God, Jesus Christ, Mary, or the saints in words or actions is called **blasphemy**.

You probably use God's name most often in prayer. Every time you make the Sign of the Cross, you call on the name of the Father, of the Son, and of the Holy Spirit. This is a reminder of your baptism. Calling on God's name strengthens you to live as a child of God and a follower of Christ.

The second commandment also reminds us that God calls each person by name. A person's name is a sign of that person's dignity. You are to use the names of others with respect.

❓ **What are some ways you use God's name?**

❓ **How can you show others that you respect their names?**

# Keeping the Lord's Day

Following the first, second, and third commandments helps you love God and grow closer to him. The third commandment teaches you to honor God by celebrating Sunday, the greatest and most special day of the week for Christians. The third commandment is this: Remember to keep holy the Lord's day.

Sunday is the first day of the week. Jesus rose from the dead on the first day of the week. This is why Sunday is known as the Lord's day. Gathering on Sunday for the Eucharist has been the center of the Church's life since the time of the Apostles. This is because Sunday is the day of the Lord's Resurrection.

## Words of Faith

**Blasphemy** is the sin of showing contempt for the name of God, Jesus Christ, Mary, or the saints in words or actions.

## The Lord's Day

- Participate in the Sunday celebration of the Eucharist. This is the most important way to observe the third commandment.

- Rest and enjoy time with your family. Share a meal, read the Bible, or visit a relative you do not often see.

- Take part in parish activities, visit a retirement center, visit people in the community who are sick, or perform a work of service as a family.

- Respect the rights of others to rest and observe Sunday.

## Activity — Connect Your Faith

**Sunday Suggestions**   What are three other actions that you could take to remember the Lord's day?

_____

_____

_____

# Think of God Every Day

 **Focus** Why are the first, second, and third commandments important?

The first three commandments are about how you act toward, think about, and worship God. They give you a guide for how you can praise God and show God respect.

## Commandments of Respect

God has given you many blessings. In return, he asks that you follow the first three commandments in worship of him. Below are some ways to show your respect for God.

**Attend Mass**
Participate in Mass every Sunday.

**Say grace**
Give thanks to God before you eat.

**Remember the meaning of religious holidays**
During the holidays, stop and think about why you are celebrating.

**Love others**
Show kindness and love to people around you. They are also made in God's image.

**Do not curse**
Pay attention to what you are saying.

**Say a prayer of thanks**
Thank God for the many blessings in your life.

**❓ What things in the church should you treat with respect?**

# Live Your Faith

**Find the Meaning**  Write the first three commandments in your own words. Then write about how you keep each commandment.

### 1st Commandment

_____

_____

_____

_____

_____

_____

_____

Journal

### 2nd Commandment

_____

_____

_____

_____

_____

_____

### 3rd Commandment

_____

_____

_____

_____

_____

_____

_____

_____

_____

# Prayer of Praise

 **Let Us Pray**

*Gather and begin with the Sign of the Cross.*

*Sing together.*

> Sing, sing, praise and sing! Honor God for ev'rything.
> Sing to God and let it ring. Sing and praise and sing!

"Sing, Sing, Praise and Sing!" © 2000, GIA Publications, Inc.

**Leader:** Respond to each name of God by praying: We praise your name, O God.

**Reader:** God, our Father,

**All:** **We praise your name, O God.**

**Reader:** All merciful and gracious God,

**All:** **We praise your name, O God.**

**Reader:** God, our Creator,

**All:** **We praise your name, O God.**

**Reader:** Compassionate God,

**All:** **We praise your name, O God.**

**Reader:** God, source of all life,

**All:** **We praise your name, O God.**

**Leader:** Let us pray.

*Bow your heads as the leader prays.*

**All:** **Amen.**

**A** **Work With Words**   Circle the word that best completes each statement.

1. Calling on God's name in (prayer/anger) helps you live as a child of God and follower of Christ.

2. (Honoring/Dishonoring) the name of God, Jesus Christ, Mary, or the saints in words or actions is called blasphemy.

3. When you adore and praise God, (except/especially) in prayer and liturgy, you are worshipping him.

4. Fortune-telling is against the (first/second) commandment.

5. When you worship God, you show your (belief/disbelief) in him as the source of creation and salvation.

**B** **Check Understanding**   Respond briefly to the following questions.

6. Who or what should you worship?

   _____

7. What did God create in his own image?

   _____

8. How can you show respect for God's name?

   _____

9. Who is called to worship at Sunday Mass?

   _____

10. What do the first three commandments tell you to do?

    _____

# Family Faith

## Catholics Believe

- The first three commandments teach you to honor God above all else, respect his name, and worship him on Sunday.

- These commandments tell you to believe in, trust, and love God.

### SCRIPTURE

Read *Psalm 119:33–48* to discover the joy you can experience by following Christ's example and living by God's law.

**GO online** www.osvcurriculum.com
For weekly scripture readings and seasonal resources

## Activity

# Live Your Faith

**Praise God** When we perform actions that show our understanding of the first three commandments, we strengthen our love for God.

- Make a list of seven actions that you and your family can do this week to praise and honor God.
- Check off the actions as you and your family move through the week, but feel free to perform these actions more than once. No one can show too much love for God.

# People of Faith

**Jane Frances de Chantal** was born into a noble family in France. She married and had seven children. When Jane became a widow, she devoted herself to the religious life. She met Francis de Sales in 1604 and grew spiritually under his guidance. Eventually, Jane founded the Order of the Visitation. These women cared for those in need. Saint Jane's feast day is December 12.

▲ Saint Jane Frances de Chantal 1572–1641

 ## Family Prayer

Saint Jane, pray for us that we may be respectful of the dignity of others and of our own dignity. Amen.

**DISCOVER**

Catholic Social
Teaching:

Rights and
Responsibilities of
the Human Person

# Faith in Action!
## CATHOLIC SOCIAL TEACHING

In this unit, you learned about the Beatitudes and the Great Commandment. These teachings of Jesus tell his followers how they should act. They are just as important today as they were in Jesus' time. Helping other people and treating them as you would like to be treated are ways you act responsibly and respect the rights of others.

## Rights and Responsibilities

God's plan is that every person should be treated with dignity. Every person, everywhere, has a right to life and to the things needed to live, such as food, clothing, shelter, and education.

With human rights come human responsibilities. Part of your mission to follow Jesus is to work for the human rights of all people. It is not fair that some people have things they do not need while others have nothing. All Christians have the responsibility to see that people everywhere are treated fairly and have what they need to live. The Catholic Church calls all of its members to find ways to fight hunger and homelessness. One way to work for human rights is to care for the needs of those who are homeless.

❷ **What human rights and responsibilities can you name?**

143

# Mealtime on the Streets

It is a winter night in Texas. People who are homeless, cold, and hungry are huddled in corners and in doorways. Suddenly, a truck appears. The doors open and people begin to give out sandwiches, hot drinks, and warm blankets. Who are these people?

This is the work of Mobile Loaves and Fishes. In the summer of 1998, six parishioners from St. John Neumann Church began planning the project. They had heard about a church that gave out blankets and coffee to the homeless, and they decided to do the same. Soon after, they distributed 75 sack lunches to citizens who were homeless.

**God calls people to share what they have with others. Let's look at what one parish did to help care for others.**

MOBILE LOAVES & FISHES
Miracles on Wheels

## A Good Idea Grows

The project grew quickly. Parishioners began to give money, volunteer their time, and offer their prayers. By spring the parish had its own truck and was distributing food seven nights a month. Soon the deliveries were up to 15 nights a month. By 2002 more than 2,000 volunteers were sending four trucks into the streets every night. In 2003 the Mobile Loaves and Fishes program served over 100,000 meals, and the project is still growing. That's what can happen when you start with an idea, a commitment, and a group of caring people!

❷ **Why do you think the project is called "Mobile Loaves and Fishes"?**

# Reach out!

## Sharing Food

One way to work for human rights is to gather food for a local food bank. Your class will have a lot to do to get ready. Check off each task as you complete it.

☐ Find a food bank nearby, and ask what kinds of foods are needed.

☐ Decide when and where you will collect the food.

☐ Decide how you will let people know about your food drive.

☐ Get containers for the food, and encourage class members to collect it.

☐ Arrange to have the food delivered to the food bank.

☐ Make cards to thank those who have donated food.

☐ Think about how to collect food other times during the year.

## Make a Difference

**Do Your Part**   Decide how you can help.

Which of the project jobs could I do best? _____

Do I have my own money that I can use to buy food? _____

Can I earn money to buy food for the poor? _____

**A** **Work with Words**   Match each description in Column 1 with the correct term in Column 2.

| Column 1 | Column 2 |
|---|---|
| _____ **1.** Loving your neighbor as yourself | **a.** Beatitudes |
| _____ **2.** The meaning of "beatitude" | **b.** charity |
| _____ **3.** The sin of showing contempt for the name of God, Jesus Christ, Mary, or the saints in words or actions | **c.** second part of the Great Commandment |
| _____ **4.** Sunday, which is the day Jesus rose from the dead | **d.** worship |
| _____ **5.** Loving God with all your heart | **e.** blessing |
| _____ **6.** Actions that care for the physical needs of others | **f.** Corporal Works of Mercy |
| _____ **7.** These tell the way to live in God's kingdom now and always. | **g.** idolatry |
| _____ **8.** To adore and praise God, especially in prayer and liturgy | **h.** Lord's day |
| _____ **9.** The virtue of love | **i.** first part of the Great Commandment |
| _____ **10.** The sin of worshipping an object or a person instead of God | **j.** blasphemy |

**B** **Check Understanding**   Complete each sentence with the correct word.

11. _____ received the Ten Commandments from God on Mount Sinai.

12. The _____ commandment says, "I am the Lord your God. You shall not have strange gods before me."

13. The _____ commandment says, "You shall not take the name of the Lord in vain."

14. The _____ commandment says, "Remember to keep holy the Lord's day."

15. The rich young man in the Scripture story could not think of selling his things and giving the _____ to the poor.

**C** **Make Connections**   Write a response to each question or statement.

16. Write an intercessory prayer for a person you know needs help.

_____

_____

17. Look at the prayer you wrote above. Which Corporal Work of Mercy would help the person for whom you prayed?

_____

18. Explain what the first three commandments teach about respect.

_____

_____

19. Explain what the Great Commandment has in common with the Corporal Works of Mercy.

_____

_____

20. What do respect and honor mean to you?

_____

_____

# Unit 4
# The Church

## In this unit you will...

learn that every person has a vocation to love and serve others. Mary and the saints are models and teachers of holiness for all of us. Jesus gave Church leaders the authority to explain Scripture and Tradition to the faithful. The Holy Spirit directs Church leaders in teaching and guiding the faithful.

Chapter 10

Chapter 11

Chapter 12

## Faith in Action!

**Catholic Social Teaching Principle:
Dignity of Work and Rights
of Workers**

# Chapter 10 Called to Love

## Let Us Pray

**Leader:** God of love, we gladly serve and obey you.

"Praise, you servants of the LORD,
praise the name of the LORD."

*Psalm 113:1*

**All:** God of love, we gladly serve and obey you. Amen.

## Activity

## Let's Begin

● **Miss Rumphius** In the story *Miss Rumphius,* a young girl named Alice Rumphius is challenged by her grandfather to make the world more beautiful. Many years later, the adult Alice discovers the lupine flower. She decides to make the fields and neighborhoods of her town more beautiful. Alice walks through the town and its fields, dropping lupine seed along her way. Now those empty lots and fields are carpets of blue every spring.

What would make the world around you a better place?

• List three ways that you can make the world around you a better place.

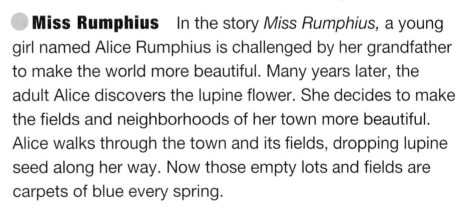

_____

_____

_____

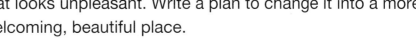

**Make a Change** Think of an area in your town or city that looks unpleasant. Write a plan to change it into a more welcoming, beautiful place.

# God's Call

 **Focus** What does it mean to have a vocation?

Everyone has a **vocation**. A vocation is God's call to love and serve him and others. Sometimes God calls a person to a special role.

Once, long before Jesus was born, there was a young man who lived in the tiny kingdom of Judah, where the nation of Israel is today. His name was Jeremiah, which means "the Lord raises up." Jeremiah was called by God to speak the truth to his people in a time of great danger. They had lost their way and were being invaded by powerful nations. This is how Jeremiah remembered God calling him.

✚ S C R I P T U R E                                        **Jeremiah 1:5–8**

## The Call of Jeremiah

"Before I formed you in the womb I knew you,
   before you were born I dedicated you, a
   prophet to the nations I appointed you.

Ah, LORD God! I said,
   I know not how to speak; 'I am too young.'

But the LORD answered me,
Say not, I am too young. . . .
whatever I command you, you shall speak.
Have no fear before them,
   because I am with you to deliver you."

From *Jeremiah 1:5–8*

❓ **Have you ever felt that God wanted you to do something or to make a certain choice?**

❓ **How did you know?**

## The Kingdom of God

Not everyone hears God's call as clearly as Jeremiah did. Sometimes it takes many years of praying and listening to know your vocation. It will be yours alone because you are a unique child of God.

All vocations can be ways of making the **kingdom of God** more visible. God's reign is the world of love, peace, and justice that God intends. Jesus announced the reign of God and revealed it in his life and ministry. But the reign of God will not be here fully until the end of time. Every person must help God increase his reign.

❓ **What signs can you see of God's kingdom in the world now?**

## Ways to Serve God

The Catholic Church recognizes three special ways in which people respond to God's call to serve: through the priesthood, through consecrated religious life, and through married life. Consecrated religious life is a state of life in which a person usually makes vows, or promises, of holiness.

## Words of Faith

A **vocation** is God's call to love and serve him and others.

The **kingdom of God** is God's rule of peace, justice, and love that is here now but has not yet come in its fullness.

## Activity

# Share Your Faith

**Reflect:** Imagine that you are much older and that a film director is preparing a movie of your life.

**Share:** Work with a partner, and pretend that your partner is the film director. Suggest two scenes that he or she could shoot to show you helping increase God's reign.

**Act:** Choose one of the scenes you described, and draw it. After you have finished drawing, write a caption for the picture.

# Serving the Church

**Focus** How do Christians help God increase his reign?

The Church recognizes that some people may choose to serve God by remaining single rather than choosing the priesthood, religious life, or married life. Single life is also a vocation. Both single and married people are part of the laity.

All who are baptized can choose to serve the Church and the parish community. Here are some of their special roles.

## Many Gifts

- The pastor and pastoral associate lead and serve the parish community.
- The permanent deacon is ordained to assist the pastor, especially at Eucharist, marriages, and funerals, and to perform works of charity.
- The lector proclaims the word of God at the Liturgy of the Word.
- The extraordinary minister of Holy Communion helps distribute Holy Communion at Mass and takes Holy Communion to those who are sick or housebound.
- Altar servers assist the priest at Mass by carrying the sacramentary, the sacred vessels, and the cross.
- Musicians lead the assembly in sung prayer.
- Catechists teach Scripture and the Catholic faith to members of the parish.

❓ Who in your family has served in one of these special roles?

❓ What other roles are there? How could you share your gifts in one of these roles?

## Using Your Gifts

It can take many years to recognize your vocation in life. However, even while you are young you can use your gifts from God to make a difference. Here is the story of a boy who used his talent to bring a powerful message to the world.

A BIOGRAPHY

# Heartsongs

Mattie Stepanek was born with a rare form of muscular dystrophy. Although he used a wheelchair and needed a machine to help him breathe, Mattie wrote beautiful poetry.

Writing poetry helped Mattie find what he called his heartsong. "Your heartsong is your inner beauty," said Mattie. "It's the song in your heart that wants you to help make yourself a better person, and to help other people do the same. Everybody has one."

## Finding Your Heartsong

Discovering your vocation is a lot like finding your heartsong. It is finding the unique way that God wants you to make the world a better place. Everyone who brings love, peace, and justice to the world helps God increase his reign.

### Activity
## Connect Your Faith

**Your Heartsong**
What could your heartsong be? Write and decorate its title in this space.

153

<br>

**Explore**

# Called by Christ

 **Focus** What does your Baptism call you to do?

Like Alice, Jeremiah, and Mattie, you too have a calling. Your call, like that of all Christians, came to you at your Baptism.

You probably do not remember your Baptism. You might have heard stories about how you cried or smiled. You know the names of your godparents. Now that you are older, you have learned more about the importance of the Sacrament of Baptism.

Through Baptism you share in Jesus' ministry as priest, prophet, and king. Here are some ways to live your baptismal commitment.

## Live Your Call

### As Priest

- Learn about God's plan for all creation.
- Pray with and for others.
- Take part in Mass.

### As Prophet

- Learn what the Church teaches about morals and justice.
- Help other people make good choices.
- Stand up for what is right, even when it is difficult to do so.

### As King

- Take responsibility for your actions and choices.
- Be a wise leader when you are with friends and younger family members.
- Follow Jesus' example by serving and forgiving others, especially those who are most in need of justice, mercy, and loving care.

**?** **When have you been a priest, prophet, or king for God?**

# Live Your Faith

**Think About Your Calling**  Design a banner or a poster about how people answer God's call. Write a slogan to accompany your artwork.

# Meditation on Peace

 Let Us Pray

*Gather and begin with the Sign of the Cross.*

**Leader:** Let us sit and listen to the words of the Letter to the Colossians.

**Reader 1:** *Read Colossians 1:2–5.*

*Silence*

*Sing together.*

Take, O take me as I am; summon out what I shall be; set your seal upon my heart and live in me.

"Take, O Take Me As I Am" © 1994, Iona Community, GIA Publications, Inc., agent

**Reader 2:** Let us reflect on peace and listen to words that Mattie Stepanek wrote about peace.

"I cannot wait to become
A peacemaker.
I cannot wait to help
The world overcome
Anger, and problems of evil."

What good things are you eager to do for the world?

**Leader:** Let us pray.

*Bow your heads as the leader prays.*

**All:** **Amen.**

**A Work with Words**   Complete the following paragraph.

**1.–5.** Jesus announced that God's _____ was at hand. By this he meant that God's reign of

_____, _____, and

_____ had begun with him, but was still to come in its fullness. All Christians are

_____ by God to cooperate with him in bringing his kingdom to fullness.

**B Check Understanding**   Fill in the circle next to the answer that best completes each statement.

**6.** The call you receive from God is known as a

_____.

○ vocation          ○ vacation          ○ commandment

**7.** _____ people who are baptized can serve a parish.

○ Some          ○ All          ○ No

**8.** _____ lead the people in prayer when they celebrate Mass.

○ Ordained deacons          ○ Parishioners          ○ Priests

**9.** Deacons do all of the following EXCEPT

_____.

○ assist at the Sacraments
○ perform works of charity
○ lead a diocese

**C Make Connections**   Complete the following statement.

**10.** Every person is called. . .

_____

_____

# Family Faith

## Catholics Believe

- **Every person is called by God to a vocation.**

- **Through your vocation, you can help God increase his reign.**

### ✝ SCRIPTURE

Read *1 Corinthians 12:1–31* to learn more about the spiritual gifts with which God blesses us.

**GO online** www.osvcurriculum.com
For weekly scripture readings and seasonal resources

## Activity

## Live Your Faith

**Name Acrostics** Sit and talk together. Discuss the gifts that you see in each member of your family. Then, using your names, create acrostics that list the gifts of your family. Here is an example:

J oyful
O thers come first
E nthusiastic

Discuss how your family members' gifts are making the world a better place.

# People of Faith

**Frédéric** was born in Milan, Italy. For a time he studied law, but in Paris he discovered a great love for literature. He had a strong faith, and his friends challenged him to find a way to live out his Christian beliefs in his everyday life. Frédéric cofounded the Society of Saint Vincent de Paul. This religious association continues today to help those in need, especially those who are poor. Blessed Frédéric's feast day is September 8.

▲ **Blessed Frédéric Ozanam 1813–1853**

##  Family Prayer

O God, help us answer your call as Blessed Frédéric did, so that we may help you increase your reign of justice, love, and peace. Amen.

# Chapter 11 Models of Faith

## Let Us Pray

**Leader:** God, help us learn from those who serve you.

"How good God is to the upright,
the Lord, to those who are clean of heart!"

*Psalm 73:1*

**All:** God, help us learn from those who serve you. Amen.

"We must be the change we wish to see."
—*Mohandas Gandhi*

"You must do the thing you think you cannot do."
—*Eleanor Roosevelt*

"I cannot help it when I see injustice. I cannot keep quiet."
—*Archbishop Desmond Tutu*

**Activity**

# Let's Begin

**● I Believe** These quotations tell you about the personal beliefs of three famous people who helped change the world. Many who make a difference are as young as you.

• What statement about your own beliefs would you like people to remember?

_____

_____

_____

• How might you act on those beliefs to change the world?

_____

_____

_____

**●Make a Poster** Design a poster that shows you making a difference in your family, school, or neighborhood.

# Holy Ones of God

 **Focus** What is faith?

The Church honors certain people whose whole lives showed others how to do God's will. These models of faith all helped God bring his reign into the world more fully. The Church calls each of these people a **saint**. Here are the stories of two of them.

A BIOGRAPHY
_____

## *Catherine of Siena*

Catherine wanted to serve God through quiet prayer. But Catherine's world was full of problems. God called her to make a difference.

Catherine lived long ago in Siena, Italy. She was very wise and used words well. Even though it was unusual for a woman of her time, Catherine made public speeches and taught priests. She also cared for those who were sick or in prison.

Catherine spoke out against injustice. She helped leaders in the Church make peace with one another. Christians learn from Catherine that every member of the Church can make a difference.

Catherine's students called her "Mother" and "Teacher." She has been named a Doctor of the Church.

## Holy Lives

Catherine of Siena is a canonized saint of the Catholic Church. This means that the Church has officially declared that she led a holy life and is enjoying eternal life with God in heaven.

❓ **What do you admire about Catherine?**

# Good Pope John

Before he was elected pope, John XXIII served soldiers who were wounded in World War I. This experience taught him to work for peace. Later he worked with religious leaders who were not Catholic. He learned to look for things that were the same in their beliefs, rather than for differences.

After he was elected pope, John XXIII called all the world's bishops to Rome to renew and reform the Catholic Church at the Second Vatican Council. He died before it ended, but the council continued. People everywhere mourned the death of the humble, friendly man they called "Good Pope John." Pope John XXIII was named blessed by the Church in September 2000 and was canonized a Saint in 2014.

❓ **What quality of Pope Saint John XXIII do you admire the most?**

## Words of Faith

A **saint** is a person who the Church declares has led a holy life and is enjoying eternal life with God in heaven.

## Activity — Share Your Faith

**Reflect:** Think about what makes Saint Catherine and Pope Saint John XXIII models of faith.

**Share:** Discuss your ideas about them with the class.

**Act:** Where the circles overlap, write what you know is true of both Saint Catherine and Pope Saint John XXIII. In the circle on the left, write what is true only for Saint Catherine. Write what is true only for Pope Saint John XXIII in the circle on the right.

**Saint Catherine**    **Pope Saint John XXIII**

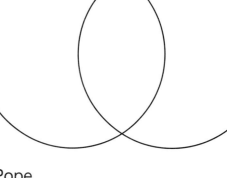

**161**

# Model of Holiness

**Focus** How is Mary a model of holiness?

There are many saints, but Mary is the perfect model of holiness. God chose Mary to be the mother of Jesus. After Mary said "yes" to being the mother of God's Son, she visited her cousin Elizabeth. Here is how Mary described her joy at the great blessing God had given her.

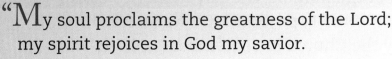

## SCRIPTURE
Luke 1: 46–50

# Mary's Song

"My soul proclaims the greatness of the Lord;
   my spirit rejoices in God my savior.
For he has looked upon his handmaid's lowliness;
   behold, from now on will all ages call
      me blessed.
The Mighty One has done great things for me,
   and holy is his name.
His mercy is from age to age
   to those who fear him."

*Luke 1:46–50*

God created Mary full of grace. He preserved her from sin from the very first moment of her conception. The Church calls this gift from God Mary's **Immaculate Conception**.

The word *immaculate* means spotless and clean—without sin. The word *conception* means the very moment when a person's life begins. The Catholic Church celebrates the Immaculate Conception of Mary on December 8.

**❓ Have you ever been given a very big responsibility? What did you say or do?**

*Madonna and Child* by Giambologna

## Your Will Be Done

Part of holiness is being able to accept and do the things that God asks of you. Mary accepted God's will throughout her life. Mary cared for and protected Jesus when he was a child. She stood by him all through his life. Mary was strong enough to be at the foot of Jesus' cross when he was crucified.

After Jesus ascended into heaven, Mary remained on earth with Jesus' followers. She was there at Pentecost when the Holy Spirit came to the disciples. Mary is called the Mother of the Church because she is an example of love and faith for Christians. Even today, she continues to hold all of her Son's followers close to her heart.

## A Guide for You

When you were baptized, you may have received the name of one of the saints of God. This person is your **patron saint**. He or she is your model of faith and prays for you from heaven. You walk in the footsteps of your saint and continue his or her good works in the way you live your life.

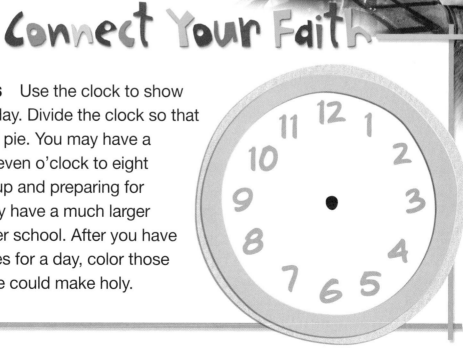

### Activity — Connect Your Faith

**Time for Holiness** Use the clock to show what you do each day. Divide the clock so that it looks like a sliced pie. You may have a narrow slice from seven o'clock to eight o'clock for getting up and preparing for school, but you may have a much larger slice for playing after school. After you have shown your activities for a day, color those that God's presence could make holy.

# Growing in Holiness

 **Focus** How can you follow the example of the saints?

Kateri Tekakwitha

Maximilian Kolbe

The Church honors saints from around the world. They have lived holy lives, and many of them have done brave things to spread God's word. You may think that you cannot be like them until you are older. All of the saints were your age once. Some saints acted heroically at a young age. There are things that you can do now.

## Let God's Love Grow

Jane Frances de Chantal

Frédéric Ozanam

In order to spread God's loving message to others, you must first allow God's love to grow within you. To do so, keep in mind the following steps.

### 1 Keep Your Eyes on Jesus

Read in the Bible about Jesus' life. When you face a problem, ask yourself how Jesus would act in that situation. Make Jesus number one in your choices and thoughts.

### 2 Read About the Lives of the Saints

Think about how these holy men and women chose to love God above everything else. Try to follow their examples of holiness.

### 3 Make Good Decisions

Follow the Ten Commandments, Jesus' law of love, and the Beatitudes. Avoid sin whenever temptation appears.

 **When have you felt God's love growing within you?**

# Live Your Faith

**Show Yourself Growing in Faith**   Create three snapshots of yourself that show ways in which you are growing in holiness.

# Litany of the Saints

 Let Us Pray

*Gather and begin with the Sign of the Cross.*

Leader: Respond with **Pray for us** after each saint's name.

Reader: Holy Mary, Mother of God

All: **Pray for us.**

Reader: Saint Michael

Saint John the Baptist

Saint Joseph

Saints Peter and Paul

Saint Mary Magdalene

Saint Stephen

Saint Agnes

Saint Gregory

Saint Francis

Saint Dominic

Saint Catherine

Saint Teresa

Saints Perpetua and Felicity

Saint Martin

Leader: Let us pray.

*Bow your heads as the leader prays.*

All: **Amen.**

 *Sing together.*

We are God's people,
the flock of the Lord.

"Psalm 100" © 1969, 1981, 1997, ICEL.

**A** **Work with Words**   Complete each sentence with the correct word from the Word Bank.

bishops
holy
mother
preserved
wisdom

1.  Catherine of Siena was named a Doctor of the Church because of her _____.

2.  Immaculate Conception is the title for Mary that recognizes that God _____ her from sin from the first moment of her life.

3.  All of the world's _____ were called to Rome for the Second Vatican Council.

4.  Mary felt great joy at being chosen by God to be the _____ of his son.

5.  A saint is recognized by the Church for living a _____ life.

**B** **Check Understanding**   Respond briefly to the following questions.

6.  How did Pope Saint John XXIII work successfully with leaders of other religions?

_____

7.  What did Mohandas Gandhi say about making a difference?

_____

8.  What did Catherine of Siena speak out against?

_____

9.  What is a patron saint?

_____

10.  What can you learn from reading about the lives of saints?

_____

# Family Faith

## Catholics Believe

- The Church's holiness shines in the saints. All who live their love of God are saints.

- Mary is the perfect model of holiness, and she is called the Mother of the Church.

### ✝ SCRIPTURE

Read *1 Thessalonians 4:13–15* for assurance that the saints are with God.

**GO online** www.osvcurriculum.com
For weekly scripture readings and seasonal resources

## Activity

# Live Your Faith

**Scrapbook** Research a patron saint for your family. You can find information about many saints in your parish library or on the Internet. Also share stories about models of holiness in your own family. Create a scrapbook with drawings and descriptions of all the models of faith you find.

# People of Faith

▲ Saint Kateri Tekakwitha 1656–1680

**Kateri Tekakwitha** is the first Native American to be canonized. She was the daughter of a Mohawk warrior and an Algonquian woman who was Christian. Kateri was born in New York in 1656 and was baptized in 1676. She devoted herself to a life of prayer, penance, and the care of those who were sick or old. After her First Communion in 1677, Kateri's devotion to the Eucharist strengthened her faith. She was canonized in 2012. Her feast day is April 17.

##  Family Prayer

O God, help us grow in holiness as Kateri did. Help us imitate her love for you and her devotion to the Eucharist. Amen.

*In Unit 4 your child is learning about the CHURCH.*

# Chapter 12 The Church Teaches

## Let Us Pray

**Leader:** God, help us follow in your faithful ways.

"Send your light and fidelity,
that they may be my guide."

*Psalm 43:3*

**All:** God, help us follow in your faithful ways.
Amen.

## Activity — Let's Begin

### ● A Good Teacher Is . . .

- someone who encourages you to think but allows you to learn from mistakes.

- someone who cares about you and what you learn.

- someone who has some truth to share.

- someone who isn't afraid to smile or cry.

Add another statement about good teachers.

_____

_____

Outside of school, who are the teachers in your life?

_____

_____

**Become a Teacher** Write a story about teaching a younger child about God's message.

# Jesus Chooses a Teacher

 **Focus** How did Jesus choose Peter as the leader of the Apostles?

The Church is your most important teacher. The Church's authority, or power to teach, was given by Jesus and is guided by the Holy Spirit. Here is a Gospel story about the beginnings of the Church's authority to teach.

## ✝ SCRIPTURE
Mark 8:27–30

# *You Are the Messiah!*

*N*ow Jesus and his disciples set out for the villages of Caesarea Philippi. Along the way he asked his disciples, "Who do people say that I am?" They said in reply, "John the Baptist, others Elijah, still others one of the prophets." And he asked them, "But who do you say that I am?" Peter said to him in reply, "You are the Messiah." Then [Jesus] warned them not to tell anyone about him.

*Mark 8:27–30*

Peter believed in Jesus and said so. Jesus gave Peter and the other Apostles a share in the authority he had from his Father. Then Jesus sent them out to preach, teach, forgive, and heal in his name.

❓ **If Jesus asked you the same question he asked Peter, what would you say?**

## Peter Denies Jesus

Peter made some mistakes along the way. Much later, at the time of Jesus' crucifixion, Peter and the other disciples were very much afraid. In fact, the night before Jesus died, Peter denied three times that he had ever known Jesus. Afterward, he was ashamed of himself and cried bitterly.

## Feed My Lambs

But Jesus never lost faith in Peter. After Jesus' death and Resurrection, Jesus was talking to Peter and the other disciples on the shore of a lake. Jesus asked three times whether Peter loved him. Of course, Peter said that he did. Jesus said to him, "Feed my lambs. Feed my sheep." See *John 21:15–17*.

In spite of Peter's earlier denials, Jesus made Peter the chief shepherd of all his flock. When he became the leader, Peter made good decisions for the members of the Church.

❓ **Why do you think Jesus asked Peter the same question three times?**

---

**Activity** — **Share Your Faith**

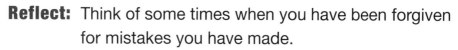

**Reflect:** Think of some times when you have been forgiven for mistakes you have made.

**Share:** During a short class prayer, mention the name of someone who has forgiven you.

**Act:** Using a separate sheet of paper, show a situation in which someone in authority gave you a second chance.

# The Church and You

 **Focus** What is your role as a member of the Church?

After Jesus ascended into heaven, Peter and all the disciples were afraid. Then on Pentecost, the Holy Spirit came and gave them courage. They went out and began to preach the good news.

The Apostles, with Peter as their head, were the first leaders of the Church. Jesus founded the Church on the Apostles. He gave them the authority to teach and lead his followers. Today the chief teachers in the Church are the pope and the bishops, the successors of the Apostles. Their authority to teach, called the **magisterium**, goes back to the authority Christ first gave to the Apostles. The Holy Spirit works through the Church's teachers to keep the whole Church faithful to the teachings of Jesus.

## Your Role

The Church's mission to share the true message of Jesus is not left to the pope and bishops alone. All members of the Body of Christ have a duty to learn Jesus' message as the Church interprets it and to share it with others. As you do this, you will grow in your love of God and neighbor.

 ❓ **Who has taught you what the Church teaches?**

# Rules for Living

Some of the responsibilities of members of the Catholic Church are summed up in the **precepts of the Church**. The Church's leaders developed these rules to show you the minimum you should do to live morally and faithfully. As a Catholic, you have a duty to live according to the teachings and precepts of the Church.

## Precepts of the Church

1. Take part in the Mass on Sundays and holy days. Keep these days holy and avoid unnecessary work.

2. Celebrate the Sacrament of Reconciliation at least once a year if you have committed a serious sin.

3. Receive Holy Communion at least once a year during Easter time.

4. Observe days of fasting and abstinence.

5. Give your time, gifts, and money to support the Church.

## Words of Faith

The **magisterium** is the Church's teaching authority to interpret the word of God found in Scripture and Tradition.

The **precepts of the Church** are some of the minimum requirements given by Church leaders for deepening your relationship with God and the Church.

## Activity — Connect Your Faith

**Word Search**  Find at least six words in this word search puzzle that relate to the teaching authority of the Church.

| F | A | I | T | H | O | P | E | A | P |
|---|---|---|---|---|---|---|---|---|---|
| B | P | R | E | C | E | P | T | S | E |
| H | O | L | Y | S | P | I | R | I | T |
| A | P | O | S | T | L | E | S | C | E |
| D | E | B | I | S | H | O | P | S | R |

Use three of these words in a sentence about your role in the Church.

_____

_____

# What You Can Give

 **Focus** How can you help support the Church?

When each person gives time, gifts, or money, the Church can provide for the needs of its members and can grow in helping meet the needs of others as well.

▶ Giving your time could include participating in any activity in which you volunteer your efforts to help with a parish event. You could work with others to decorate the church for a special liturgy, or you could donate time to the nursery during Sunday Mass or a parish meeting.

▶ Sharing your gifts or talents with the Church community is also important. You could sing in the children's choir or make banners for a school Mass.

▶ Giving your money supports the work of the parish, such as ministering to those who are in need. Money is needed to purchase food and other supplies for shelters. It is also needed to run the parish. For example, the parish has to pay for electricity, water, and heat. Even if your allowance or other income is small, you should give what you can to your parish.

❓ **How might you use your time, talent, or money for the Church?**

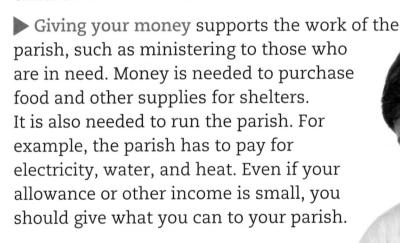

# Live Your Faith

**Write a Story** Write a story about a time when you gave your time, talent, or money to help the Church. Be sure to include how you felt afterward.

_____

_____

_____

_____

_____

_____

_____

_____

_____

_____

_____

_____

_____

_____

_____

# Prayer to the Holy Spirit

**Let Us Pray**

*Gather and begin with the Sign of the Cross.*

*Sing together the refrain.*

Come Lord Jesus,
send us your Spirit,
renew the face of the earth.
Come Lord Jesus,
send us your Spirit,
renew the face of the earth.

"Send Us Your Spirit" © 1981, 1982, 1987, GIA Publications, Inc.

**The Pentecost** by Juan de Juanes

**Group 1:** Come, Holy Spirit, fill the hearts of your faithful. And kindle in them the fire of your love.

**All:** *Sing refrain.*

**Group 2:** Send forth your Spirit and they shall be created. And you shall renew the face of the earth.

**All:** *Sing refrain.*

Lord, by the light of the Holy Spirit you have taught the hearts of your faithful. In the same Spirit, help us desire what is right and always rejoice in your consolation. We ask this through Christ our Lord. Amen.

**Leader:** Let us pray.

*Bow your heads as the leader prays.*

**All:** Amen.

**Celebrate**

**A** **Work with Words**   Complete each sentence with the correct word from the Word Bank.

| WORD BANK |
|---|
| precepts |
| Holy Spirit |
| authority |
| live according to |
| magisterium |

1. Some of the rules that the Church gives to help you grow closer to Jesus are called the _____ of the Church.

2. Jesus gave the Church the _____ to teach and lead the Body of Christ.

3. You have the duty to _____ the rules and laws of the Church.

4. The _____ is the teaching authority of the Church.

5. The Church and the magisterium are guided by the _____.

**B** **Check Understanding**   Circle True if a statement is true, and circle False if a statement is false. Correct any false statements.

6. Only wealthy people can help support the Church.
   True     False   _____

7. On Christmas the Holy Spirit came and gave the disciples courage to go out and preach the good news.
   True     False   _____

8. The pope and bishops are the chief teachers in the Church.
   True     False   _____

9. When John became the leader of the Church, he made good decisions for the members.
   True     False   _____

10. Jesus sent the Apostles out to preach, teach, forgive, and heal in his name.
    True     False   _____

# Family Faith

## ◎ Catholics Believe

■ Jesus gave the leaders of the Church the authority to interpret Scripture and Tradition for the faithful.

■ The Holy Spirit directs the Church in teaching and guiding the People of God.

### ✝ SCRIPTURE

Read *Nehemiah 8:1–12* to see how the ancient Israelites kept the Sabbath.

**GO online** www.osvcurriculum.com
For weekly scripture readings and seasonal resources

## Activity

# Live Your Faith

**Sunday Suggestions** As a family, choose ways to observe the Church precept to keep Sunday holy. Create a list of *dos* and *don'ts*. For example:

- **Do** go to Mass.
- **Do** visit relatives.
- **Do** have a family picnic.
- **Don't** spend the day shopping at the mall.
- **Don't** make sports more important than God.

Encourage one another to practice these suggestions on the next Sunday. Discuss the experience.

# People of Faith

▲ Saint Mary Magdalen Postel 1756–1846

**Mary Magdalen Postel** was educated in a Benedictine convent, where she dedicated herself to God. At eighteen she opened a school for girls in France just before the French Revolution broke out. During the revolution her school was closed, and Mary Magdalen became a leader who sheltered fugitive priests. After the revolution Mary Magdalen Postel continued to work in the field of religious education. Her teachings became well known. Saint Mary Magdalen's feast day is July 16.

##  Family Prayer

Saint Mary Magdalen, pray for us that we may open our hearts and minds to learn more as we grow in faith and in our love for God. Amen.

*In Unit 4 your child is learning about the* CHURCH.

DISCOVER

Catholic Social
Teaching:

The Dignity of
Work and the
Rights of Workers

# Faith in Action!
## CATHOLIC SOCIAL TEACHING

In this unit, you learned that every person has gifts and talents, or special skills and abilities. One way to show God that you are thankful for these gifts is to use them to help others. As a follower of Jesus, you can use your talents to make the world a better place for everyone.

## The Dignity of Work

Work is more than just a way to make money or complete a task—God calls you to discover your unique gifts and talents and to use them in your work. When you do this, your work becomes part of God's continuing work of creation. Through work, people can see that they have dignity as gifted children of God.

**❓ When have you used your gifts and talents along with others?**

## Respecting All Workers

One kind of work is no more important than another. Each person's work can help his or her community and the people who live there. How much a job pays is not important. Every worker and every kind of work is important and worthy of respect.

**❓ What kinds of work do you respect most? Why?**

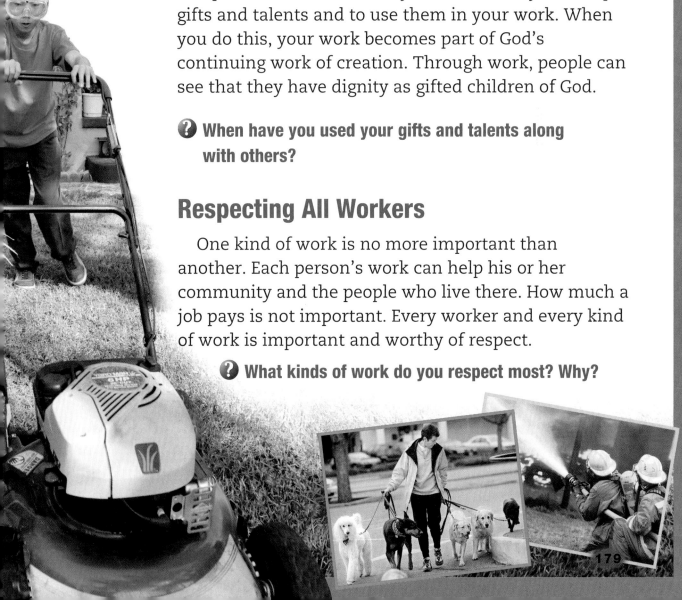

# A School of Talents

At St. Charles School in Indiana, students use the talents God gave them to work together on an art project. Students also learn that an important part of working together is respecting the abilities of the people with whom they are working.

God has given all of his people talents and abilities. Let's look at how one Catholic school is helping its students learn to respect these gifts in one another.

## Together Is Better

Each year, students in the third through sixth grades combine their talents to change the art room into a different place. Groups of students work together on many tasks to help complete the project. They decide the theme, plan the project, make the scenery, and invite guests to tour the room when it is done.

One year the students created a tropical rain forest, complete with their own plants and animals. In another year, the art room became an Egyptian tomb. Students at St. Charles School learn that they are important workers. Their project could never be completed without planners, artists, writers, and designers. The students at St. Charles know that they are gifted by God and deserve one another's respect and cooperation.

❓ **What do the students learn during their project?**

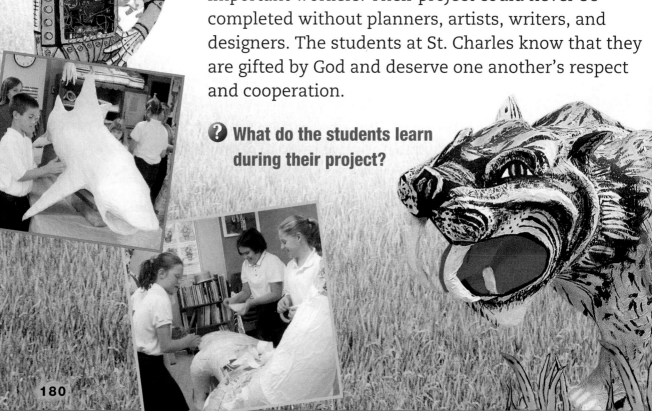

# Reach Out!

## Design a Space

In small groups, plan, design, and create a fun bulletin board for your classroom. Each student will take part in the project, according to his or her interest and talents.

The theme of our bulletin board will be _____
_____

The materials we will need are
_____
_____

The bulletin board will be designed by _____
_____

The art for the bulletin board will be made by _____
_____
_____

The bulletin board message will be written by _____
_____
_____

The bulletin board will be put together by _____
_____

## Make a Difference

**Display Your Talents**    After the bulletin board is complete, share it with another class or invite your families to see it. Then describe to your guests how you worked together and which talents everyone used.

# UNIT 4 REVIEW

**A** **Work with Words**   Solve the puzzle with terms from the Word Bank.

**WORD BANK**

| vocation | canonization | kingdom | laity |
| conception | saint | patron saint | |
| magisterium | precepts | altar server | |

## Down

1. A _____ is God's call to serve him and others.

2. God's _____ is here now, but has not yet come in its fullness.

3. Observing days of fasting and abstinence is one of the _____ of the Church.

4. The Church's teaching authority to interpret Scripture and Tradition

6. The Immaculate _____ is the teaching that Mary was preserved from sin from the first moment of her life.

7. A person who the Church declares has lead a holy life and is enjoying life with God in heaven

## Across

5. Assists the priest at Mass

8. The process by which the Church officially declares someone a saint

9. A model of faith and a protector for you

10. All the baptized who are not priests or religious brothers or sisters

**B** **Check Understanding** Complete each sentence with the correct word from the Word Bank.

**WORD BANK**

holiness

magisterium

call

members

bishops

11. In the story of Catherine of Siena, you learned that Catherine followed God's _____.

12. Pope Saint John XXIII called all of the world's _____ to Rome to renew and reform the Catholic Church at the Second Vatican Council.

13. Mary is the perfect model of _____.

14. All _____ of the Church have a duty to learn Jesus' message and share it with others.

15. The _____ is the Church's authority to teach.

**C** **Make Connections** Write a response to each question or statement.

16. Through Baptism you share in Jesus' ministry as priest, prophet, and king. Think about the stories of Jesus in the Bible. Describe a story that shows Jesus acting as a priest, a prophet, or a king.

_____

_____

17. Name two ways in which you can grow in holiness today.

_____

18. Explain how supporting the Church by offering your time, gifts, and money strengthens the Church community.

_____

_____

19. Why is Mary so important to Christians?

_____

_____

20. Explain the Church's role as a teacher.

_____

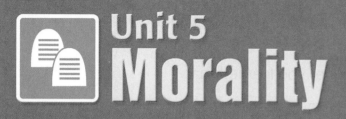

# Unit 5
# Morality

## In this unit you will...

learn that all human life is sacred. God created humans to live in strong, loving families and communities. These communities are called to respect life and live in the truth. We learn basic ways of respecting human life by practicing the Fourth through Tenth Commandments.

Chapter 13

Chapter 14

Chapter 15

## Faith in Action!

**Catholic Social Teaching Principle:**
**Solidarity of the Human Family**

# Chapter 13 Family Love

## Let Us Pray

**Leader:** God, may we always share your happiness with those we love.

"Happy are all who fear the LORD, who walk in the ways of God."

*Psalm 128:1*

**All:** God, may we always share your happiness with those we love. Amen.

## Activity

### Let's Begin

● **All Shapes and Sizes**   God loves each family, no matter what its shape or size. He wants each family member to be a sign of his love within the family.

Now think about who in your family has shown you God's love.

• List things you do to share God's love with your family.

_____

_____

_____

● **Create a Photo Album**   Create a photo album of your family. Draw each person, and write about how he or she shares God's love.

# Families in God's Plan

**Focus** What makes families strong?

God's plan for humans includes living in families. The following story shares an important lesson about living as a family.

**A FABLE**

## The Bundle of Sticks

Some brothers and sisters were quarreling among themselves, so their father asked them to bring him a handful of sticks. He tied the sticks together in a bundle. Then the father placed the bundle in the hands of each child in turn and said, "Break it into pieces." None of the children could break the bundle.

Then the father separated the sticks and handed one to each child. The children broke the individual sticks easily. Their father told them, "If you are divided among yourselves, you will be broken as easily as these individual sticks. But if you unite to help one another, you will be strong, like the bundle of sticks. You will not be overcome by attempts to divide you."

Based on an Aesop fable

❓ **What is the lesson of this fable? Name a time when your family has learned the same lesson.**

# Family Unity

God created humans to live in families. Like the father in the story, God wants families to be strong, to protect one another, and to live in peace and love.

The fourth, sixth, and ninth commandments provide basic laws about family love and respect. The fourth commandment is this: Honor your father and mother. Jesus is the perfect example for living out this commandment.

## ✝ SCRIPTURE                    Luke 2:41–52

# Jesus and His Family

When Jesus was twelve, he went to Jerusalem with his family to celebrate Passover. As Mary and Joseph were returning home, they realized that Jesus was not with them. They finally found him talking with the teachers in the Temple. Mary told Jesus how worried they had been, and Jesus returned to Nazareth with his parents.

Jesus was obedient as he grew in wisdom and age. His actions were pleasing to God and to all who knew him.

Based on *Luke 2:41–52*

❓ **When has it been difficult to obey your parents? Why?**

## Activity — Share Your Faith

**Reflect:** What keeps a family strong and close?

**Share:** Talk about these things in a group.

**Act:** Imagine that your group is working on a new TV series about families. Come up with a name for the series and titles for three episodes.

# Commandments for Families

 **Focus** What do the commandments teach about family love?

The fourth commandment teaches you to honor your parents and guardians. You honor them when you

- listen to and **obey** them in all that is good.
- show gratitude for all that they do for you.
- respect and care for them as they grow older.
- respect people in authority.

Parents and guardians provide for your needs, serve as good role models, and share their faith with you. They help you grow in faith, make good choices, and decide your vocation.

## Faith Fact

About 260,000 Catholic marriages are celebrated each year in the United States.

## Faithful Love

The sixth commandment is this: You shall not commit adultery. The ninth is this: You shall not covet your neighbor's wife. These commandments are about the faithful love and commitment between married couples.

When a man and woman marry, they make solemn promises called **vows**. They promise to love and honor each other always and to welcome the gift of children.

Part of being faithful is respecting the vows of other married couples and not acting in ways that could weaken their marriage. Adultery means being unfaithful to these vows. The grace of the Sacrament of Matrimony strengthens the couple to be faithful and true.

❓ **What does it mean to be a good role model? Who has been a good role model for you?**

## Faithfulness and You

The sixth and ninth commandments apply to everyone. You can live out these commandments by keeping promises to family, friends, and God. You can practice **modesty** by dressing, talking, and acting in ways that honor your own dignity and that of others. You can respect that the differences between males and females are gifts from God.

## Family Disappointments

Sometimes it is hard for families to live as God intends. Arguments, hurts, and disappointments can keep families from being signs of God's love. Parents and children sometimes hurt one another. Some families are hurt through separation, divorce, or even death.

But God continues to love all families and to help them grow stronger. Every time families are signs of love, they reflect the love that exists within the Holy Trinity.

❓ **What can families do to be signs of God's love?**

### Words of Faith

To **obey** is to do things or act in certain ways that are requested by those in authority.

**Vows** are solemn promises that are made to or before God.

**Modesty** is the virtue that helps people dress, talk, and act in appropriate ways.

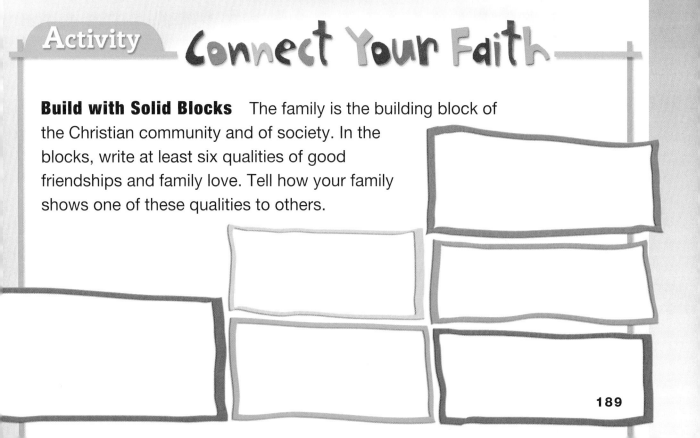

**Activity** Connect Your Faith

**Build with Solid Blocks**   The family is the building block of the Christian community and of society. In the blocks, write at least six qualities of good friendships and family love. Tell how your family shows one of these qualities to others.

# Loving Others

**Focus** How can you follow God's commandments in your family life?

God asks you to show his love to your family at all times. This is not always easy, but keeping the fourth, sixth, and ninth commandments will help you.

## Ways to Show God's Love

💜 Practice modesty by dressing decently and by avoiding television programs, movies, books, and music that show disrespect for God's gift of sexuality.

💜 Don't be jealous of other family members. Include others in your friendships.

💜 Remember that being part of a family means forgiving one another as God forgives people when they sin.

💜 Respect, honor, and obey your parents and other family members. Listen to them, and pay attention to their needs.

💜 Keep the promises you make to your family, friends, and God. Do what you have said you will do.

💜 Share your possessions, your time, and your gifts with family members.

❓ **How will following the commandments make your family life better?**

**Choose Loving Actions**   Below are situations in which you could find yourself. Write what you would do in each situation. Your answer should give an example of how you act to share God's love and follow his commandments.

Next, think about how hard it will be for you to remember to behave this way in your life. On the line above the story, draw stars to show how easy or difficult it will be to behave in the way that you have written.

- If the correct way to behave is easy, give it ⭐
- If the situation is difficult, give it ⭐⭐
- If the situation is very difficult, give it ⭐⭐⭐

You are playing a video or computer game, and you have reached the highest level you have ever achieved. Just as you begin the new level, you hear your mother calling you. It is your turn to set the table for dinner.

_____
_____
_____
_____

Your entire family has gathered at your grandmother's house for Easter. As you are playing with your cousin, you accidentally break a vase. There are no adults in the room, and your cousin wants to throw away the pieces and not tell anyone.

_____
_____
_____
_____

You are at a friend's house watching TV. A show comes on that you know your parents would not let you watch. The people on the show are using bad language.

_____
_____
_____
_____

# Prayer of Petition

 **Let Us Pray**

*Gather and begin with the Sign of the Cross.*

**Leader:** God, from you every family learns to love. We ask you to strengthen our families.

**All:** **Hear us, O Lord.**

**Reader 1:** May parents and those who care for us be blessed in their commitment to love their children and each other.

**All:** **Hear us, O Lord.**

**Reader 2:** May all children find support and security in their families.

**All:** **Hear us, O Lord.**

**Reader 3:** May all families discover your gift of faithful love.

**All:** **Hear us, O Lord.**

**Leader:** Let us pray.

*Bow your heads as the leader prays.*

**All:** **Amen.**

*Sing together.*

All grownups, all children,
all mothers, all fathers
are sisters and brothers
in the fam'ly of God.

"All Grownups, All Children"
© 2000, GIA Publications, Inc.

**A** **Work with Words**   Complete the following paragraph with the correct words from the Word Bank.

**WORD BANK**

faithful
fourth
families
sixth
honor

**1–5.** God made humans to live as _____ who love and respect one another. By following the _____ commandment, children _____ and obey their parents and guardians. The _____ and ninth commandments are about being _____ in marriage and keeping promises.

**B** **Check Understanding**   Write a definition for each of the following words.

**6.** Obey: _____

_____

**7.** Vows: _____

_____

**8.** Modesty: _____

_____

**9.** Adultery: _____

_____

**10.** Faithful: _____

_____

# Family Faith

## Catholics Believe

- God created humans to live in strong, loving families.

- The fourth, sixth, and ninth commandments provide basic laws of family love and respect.

### ✝ SCRIPTURE

Read *Galatians 6:9–10* to find out about love in the family of faith.

**GO online** www.osvcurriculum.com
For weekly scripture readings and seasonal resources

## Activity

# Live Your Faith

**Make Coupons** Discuss with your family something you shared with your class this week. Then talk about the importance of showing love to one another. Make coupons that can be given to family members at appropriate times.

Example:

~ COUPON ~
Good for one hug.

# People of Faith

Little is known about the parents of Mary. Legend says that **Anne** and **Joachim** had wanted a child for a long time. When Mary was born, they took her to the Temple and dedicated her to God. Anne and Joachim raised Mary to respect others, to be faithful to God, and to follow God's ways in all things. Saint Anne is the patron of women who are childless and women who are pregnant. Saint Anne is often pictured teaching Mary to read. The feast day of Saints Anne and Joachim is July 26.

▲ Saints Anne and Joachim
first century B.C.

 ## Family Prayer

Saints Anne and Joachim, pray for our families, that we may become signs of God's loving and forgiving presence to one another and to the world. Amen.

# Chapter 14 Choosing Life

## Let Us Pray

**Leader:** God, we thank you for your precious gifts of life and light.

"For with you is the fountain of life, and in your light we see light."

*Psalm 36:10*

**All:** God, we thank you for your precious gifts of life and light. Amen.

**Activity**  Let's Begin

### If I Can Stop One Heart from Breaking

If I can stop one heart from breaking,
I shall not live in vain;
If I can ease one life the aching,
Or cool one pain,
Or help one fainting robin
Unto his nest again,
I shall not live in vain.

Emily Dickinson

• Write a short poem about how you will make your life worthwhile.

_____

_____

_____

_____

• **Spread the Message** Create a collage that promotes life and happiness for others.

195

# Respect Life

 **Focus** How do you respect life?

Living a worthwhile life means respecting and caring for others' lives. Here is a true story about a man who made a choice to respect life.

BIOGRAPHY

## A CHANGE OF HEART

About eighty years ago Alfred Nobel picked up the morning paper and, to his horror, read his own death notice! The newspaper had reported his death by mistake. Nobel read the bold heading, "Dynamite King Dies." In the article he was described as a merchant of death.

Nobel was saddened. Although he had made a fortune by inventing dynamite, he did not want to be remembered as a "merchant of death." From then on, he devoted his energy and money to works of peace and the good of humankind.

Today, Alfred Nobel is remembered as the founder of the Nobel Prizes, especially the Peace Prize. These prizes reward and encourage people who work for the good of others.

❓ **If your death notice were written accidentally today, what could it say about your respect for the lives of others?**

Nobel Peace Prize winners

# The Fifth Commandment

Alfred Nobel changed the direction of his life and began supporting work that gave life to others. He was a clear example of respect for the fifth commandment: You shall not kill.

All human life is sacred, and all actions that support and protect life support the fifth commandment. At the end of his life Moses told the people to remember that God's law was life for them.

## SCRIPTURE

I call heaven and earth today to witness against you: I have set before you life and death, the blessing and the curse. Choose life, then, that you and your descendants may live, by loving the LORD, your God, heeding his voice, and holding fast to him. For that will mean life for you. . . .

*Deuteronomy 30:19–20*

## A Path to Life

God's laws show the path to life and happiness. The fifth commandment reminds you of the fundamental respect for life that is owed to every person. Because every life comes from God, every human life is sacred from the moment of conception until the time of death.

## Activity — Share Your Faith

**Reflect:** Think about someone you know who deserves a prize for the way that he or she respects life.

**Share:** Share with a partner what this person does to respect life.

**Act:** Design a medal to honor the person you chose. Write his or her name on the line.

# Keeping the Fifth Commandment

 **Focus** How do you keep the fifth commandment?

All human life is sacred, including the life of the unborn and the elderly. The life of an unborn child is most fragile, and it is deserving of the greatest respect and care. Thus, the intentional ending of the life of an unborn child is a grave sin.

The taking of one's own life is suicide. It is seriously contrary to God's gift of life and love. However, one's responsibility may be lessened by certain factors. **Murder**, the intentional killing of an innocent person, is seriously sinful because it contradicts Jesus' law of love. To kill in self-defense, however, is justified, if it is the only way to protect one's own life.

The Catholic Church teaches that the death penalty, or capital punishment, is almost always wrong. Alternatives, such as life in prison without parole, are preferred.

## Respect for the Body

The Church teaches that your body and soul are united. You are a temple in which God's Spirit dwells. The fifth commandment teaches you to respect your body and those of others. Eating healthful foods and getting enough exercise are important to protect your life and health. At your age, using alcohol is an offense against the fifth commandment. The use of tobacco and illegal drugs is harmful to the body. Tempting or encouraging others to disrespect the gift of life is wrong, too.

❓ **What can you do to help others respect life?**

## Jesus' Message

Jesus said that even anger can be sinful if it is not controlled; anger can harden into hatred. Hatred can lead to revenge, or getting back at someone for something that has happened, or to violence.

It can be difficult to show love and respect for those who bully or treat you unfairly. Jesus calls you to love in this way.

### Words of Faith

**Murder** is the intentional killing of an innocent person.

---

### ✝ SCRIPTURE                    Matthew 5:43–45

## Love of Enemies

You have heard that it was said, "You shall love your neighbor and hate your enemy." But I say to you, love your enemies, and pray for those who persecute you, that you may be children of your heavenly Father, for he makes his sun rise on the bad and the good, and causes rain to fall on the just and unjust.

*Matthew 5:43–45*

❓ **What did Jesus mean when he said that God makes his sun rise on the bad and the good?**

---

## Activity — Connect Your Faith

**Choose Life**   Circle one life-giving action that you will practice today.

- Protect unborn children.
- Let go of anger.
- Forgive your enemies.
- Set a good example for others.
- Show respect for your body by eating healthful foods.

# Apply the Fifth Commandment

 **Focus** How can you act in the spirit of the fifth commandment?

The fifth commandment may seem easy to follow. But as you have read, there is more to this commandment than not killing. The commandment also asks that you take care of and respect yourself and others.

Here are some ways to show God that you respect life and are following the fifth commandment.

**Respect life** by treating younger children and babies with patience and kindness.

**Do not fight,** but learn to compromise.

**Don't bully** or make fun of others.

**Learn tolerance** by getting to know someone who seems different.

**Make peace** with those who have hurt you.

**Avoid risks** that might lead you or others to be hurt.

**Seek forgiveness** from those whom you have hurt.

**Control your anger** by releasing it in a physical activity or by talking to someone you trust.

❓ **What have you done this week to follow the fifth commandment?**

# Live Your Faith

**Practice Forgiveness** Write two letters that show how you are following God's fifth commandment. One letter should be a letter of forgiveness to someone who has treated you unfairly. The second letter should be a letter to someone you have treated unfairly, asking that person to forgive you.

# Celebration of the Word

 **Let Us Pray**

*Gather and begin with the Sign of the Cross.*

**Reader 1:** A reading from the First Letter of Peter.

*Read 1 Peter 3:9–12.*

The word of the Lord.

**All:** **Thanks be to God.**

**Reader 2:** When we are given the choice to walk away or to stay and fight,

**All:** **Help us choose your way, O Lord.**

**Reader 3:** When we are given the choice to stay angry or to forgive,

**All:** **Help us choose your way, O Lord.**

**Reader 4:** When we are given the chance to help those who are sick, disabled, or elderly,

**All:** **Help us choose your way, O Lord.**

**Leader:** Let us pray.

*Bow your heads as the leader prays.*

**All:** **Amen.**

*Sing together.*

Jesu, Jesu, fill us with your love, show us how to serve the neighbors we have from you.

"Jesu, Jesu." © 1969, Hope Publishing Co.

**A** **Work with Words**   Complete the following statements.

1. The fifth commandment says this:

   _____.

2. Every human life is a gift from _____.

3. One serious sin against the fifth commandment is

   _____.

4. All human life is _____.

5. Hatred can lead to _____.

**B** **Check Understanding**   Complete each sentence with the correct term from the Word Bank.

**WORD BANK**

Nobel Prizes
anger
wrong
enemies

6. After reading an article about his death, Alfred Nobel changed his life and founded the _____.

7. Jesus said to love everyone, even your

   _____.

8. Tempting or encouraging others to disrespect the gift of life is _____.

9. Jesus explained that uncontrolled

   _____ is against the fifth commandment.

**C** **Make Connections**   Write a brief response to the statement.

10. Explain one way that you can follow the fifth commandment.

    _____

    _____

# Family Faith

## Catholics Believe

- All human life is sacred because it comes from God.

- The fifth commandment forbids anything that takes a human life.

 **SCRIPTURE**

Read *Isaiah 9:1–6* to find out about the Prince of Peace.

GO online **www.osvcurriculum.com**
For weekly scripture readings and seasonal resources

## Activity

# Live Your Faith

**Write a Letter of Thanks**  Research the life and work of a recent Nobel Peace Prize winner who is still alive. Find out about the person's contribution and how he or she has worked for peace. Write a letter to the person, thanking him or her for choosing life.

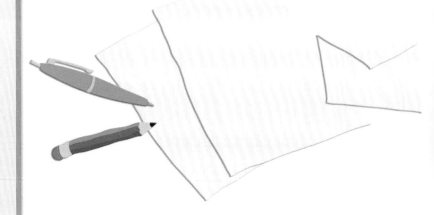

# People of Faith

**Maximilian Kolbe** was ordained a Franciscan priest and was devoted to Our Lady of the Immaculate Conception. During World War II he was imprisoned at Auschwitz. While in prison, Maximilian encouraged other prisoners to hold fast to God's love. He volunteered to take the place of a young father condemned to execution by the Nazis. He chose life even as he gave his own for another. Maximilian was named a saint in 1982. His feast day is August 14.

▲ Saint Maximilian Kolbe
1894–1941

## Family Prayer

Saint Maximilian Kolbe, pray for us that we may be faithful to God's love and always choose the path of life and hope. Amen.

# Chapter 15 Live in Truth

 **Let Us Pray**

**Leader:** Lord God, may we always be honest in our praise of you.

"Teach me, LORD, your way
   that I may walk in your truth,"

*Psalm 86:11*

**All:** Lord God, may we always be honest in our praise of you.
Amen.

Honesty is the best policy.
I cannot tell a lie.
The truth will set you free.

**Activity** Let's Begin

● **It's the Truth!** Look at the sayings on the board. Then create your own saying about the importance of telling the truth.

Now think about why people sometimes do not tell the truth. What are some reasons they give for lying?

_____

_____

_____

✎ **Write a Skit** Write a skit about a person who learns that being dishonest leads to trouble.

205

# Honest Choices

 **Focus** How do people witness to the truth?

Thomas More, an important official in England in the sixteenth century, was imprisoned for refusing to tell a lie. Thomas had an important decision to make. In a letter to his daughter, he discussed his dilemma.

### A LETTER

# THOMAS MORE

My dearest Meg,

Your father greets you with all his affection but not much hope. The dilemma I face will not soon go away.

I have been imprisoned now for some months. All I have to do to be set free is to take the Oath of Supremacy. But how can I?

If I take the oath, I will be saying that Henry VIII is the supreme head of the Catholic Church in England. You know that my Catholic faith is strong, and I believe that the pope is the true head of the Catholic Church.

King Henry is angry. He is afraid that if I go against him, other people will follow my example. I am being forced to make a choice: be honest and be killed, or tell a lie and live.

Pray for me.
Your loving father,

Thomas More

❓ **Have you ever had to decide whether to speak the truth, tell a lie, or remain silent? What happened?**

# Living the Truth

Thomas More chose to remain true to his beliefs and speak the truth. As a result, the king had him killed, but the Catholic Church named him a saint. Many saints and heroes have suffered torture and death for the sake of the truth of their faith. A person who stays faithful to Christ and suffers and dies rather than denying the truth is called a **martyr**. Martyrs live the truth by backing up their words with actions.

You probably will not be called on to be a martyr. But every follower of Jesus is called to live in the truth. By your actions you show your faithfulness to Jesus and the truth of his message.

## Words of Faith

A **martyr** is someone who gives up his or her life to witness to the truth of the faith.

## Activity

### Share Your Faith

Truth-telling

**Reflect:** Think about why it is always best to tell the truth.

**Share:** With a partner, list ten reasons for truth-telling.

**Act:** List words for a song about truth-telling.

_____   _____   _____

# The Eighth Commandment

 **Focus** What does the eighth commandment call you to do?

God is the source of all truth. His word and his law call people to live in the truth. The eighth commandment says this: You shall not bear false witness against your neighbor.

The eighth commandment forbids lying, or purposely not telling the truth. Lying can take many forms. If a person lies in court when under oath, he or she commits perjury, or false witness. Gossip is talking about another person behind his or her back. Gossip may or may not be a lie, but all gossip can harm the good reputation of another person.

All lies are unjust and unloving. All require **reparation**, or repair. Reparation may be as simple as an apology, or it may take more work, such as trying to help a person get back the reputation you have hurt.

❷ **What are some ways you can repair the damage to another person when you have not told the truth?**

# Jesus Is the Truth

Living in the spirit of the eighth commandment is more than not lying. You must choose to be truthful in words and actions. When you are truthful, you are living as a follower of Jesus, who always told the truth.

## SCRIPTURE

John 8:31–32, 14:6

### The Truth Will Set You Free

Jesus . . . said . . . , "If you remain in my word, you will truly be my disciples, and you will know the truth, and the truth will set you free. . . . I am the way and the truth and the life. No one comes to the Father except through me."

*John 8:31–32, 14:6*

People trusted what Jesus did and said. When you are truthful, people trust you. When you promise to tell the truth, you have a special duty. Let your "yes" mean "yes" and your "no" mean "no." Telling the truth will set you free to follow Jesus and to live in love.

## Words of Faith

**Reparation** is action taken to repair the damage done by sin.

## Activity

# Connect Your Faith

**Live the Truth** Read the following list, and mark an X if a statement talks about living in truth and an O if it does not. For each statement marked with an O, tell one way the person could make up for his or her wrong choice.

_____ Juanita heard an unkind story about a classmate. She did not repeat it.

_____ Scott bragged falsely about how good he was at sports.

_____ Samantha told her parents that she was going to the library, but instead she went to the park.

_____ Maria discovered that her friend had shoplifted. Maria did not tell her other friends.

209

# The Eighth Commandment in Your Life

 **Focus** How can you live in the spirit of the eighth commandment?

Sometimes being honest can be difficult. It is never easy to admit to having done something wrong when you know that you may be punished. But being honest with others and yourself is what God asks of you in the eighth commandment.

## Choose Honesty and Truth

Imagine what your life would be like if no one trusted you. No friend would tell you a secret. No one would believe anything that you said.

Sounds lonely, doesn't it? Besides, dishonesty is against God's law, and it can lead to hurting others.

### Choose the Truth

- Use words that show respect for other people.

- Do not gossip or tell lies about someone else.

- Make sure that your actions reflect your true self. Don't exaggerate, brag, or act better than others.

- Tell the truth, especially when you have promised to do so.

- Do not spread rumors about others.

- Avoid being prejudiced against those who are different.

❓ **Has anyone ever been dishonest with you? How did it make you feel?**

# Live Your Faith

**Choose a Mascot for Truth**   Sports teams, schools, and businesses have mascots such as animals, people, or items found in nature. A mascot represents a quality that a team or company has and wants people to remember.

Below are three mascots and the team or company that chose each one. What qualities do you think each mascot is supposed to represent? Write your answer below each picture.

The Tigers
Soccer Team

_____

_____

Mike's Delivery
Service

_____

_____

Johnson
Elementary School

_____

_____

Draw your own mascot to represent your choice to live an honest and truthful life. On the lines below, explain your choice.

_____

_____

_____

_____

_____

_____

_____

_____

# Prayer of Petition

 Let Us Pray

*Gather and begin with the Sign of the Cross.*

**Leader:** Whenever we are afraid to tell the truth,

**All:** **Spirit of Truth, guide us!**

**Leader:** Whenever we are tempted to gossip,

**All:** **Spirit of Truth, guide us!**

**Leader:** Whenever we are faced with choices about telling the truth,

**All:** **Spirit of Truth, guide us!**

**Leader:** Whenever we falsely judge another,

**All:** **Spirit of Truth, guide us!**

**Leader:** God of all truth, whenever we face choices about telling the truth, guide us to your light. Give us strength to make good choices. We ask this in Jesus' name. Amen.

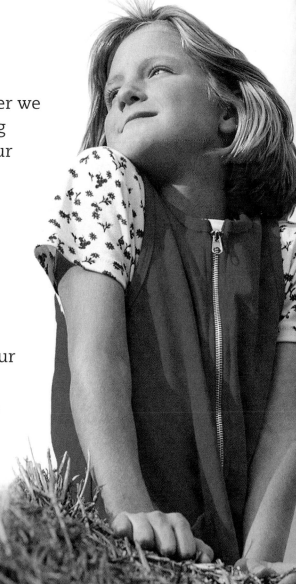

*Sing together.*

Send down the fire of your justice, Send down the rains of your love; Come, send down the Spirit, breathe life in your people, and we shall be people of God.

"Send Down the Fire" ©2001, GIA Publications, Inc.

**A** **Work with Words**   Fill in the circle next to the answer that best completes each statement.

1. A _____ is someone who gives up his or her life to witness to Jesus and the truth of the faith.

   ○ priest          ○ deacon          ○ martyr

2. _____ are sins against the eighth commandment.

   ○ lying and gossip   ○ stealing and lying   ○ gossip and murder

3. _____ is making up for a hurt or repairing a wrong.

   ○ Perjury         ○ Sin             ○ Reparation

4. The eighth commandment is "You shall not _____."

   ○ kill
   ○ bear false witness against your neighbor
   ○ keep holy the Lord's day

5. _____ are called to live in truth.

   ○ Only martyrs
   ○ Only priests and deacons
   ○ All Christians

**B** **Check Understanding**   Complete each sentence with the correct word from the Word Bank.

| WORD BANK |
| --- |
| martyr |
| unloving |
| lying |
| truth |
| gossip |

6. Jesus calls you to live in the _____.

7. Thomas More was a _____ and a saint.

8. _____ is purposely not telling the truth.

9. _____ is talking about another person behind his or her back.

10. All lies are unjust and _____.

# Family Faith

## Live Your Faith

### Catholics Believe

- Because God is truth, his people are called to live in the truth.

- The eighth commandment forbids lying.

### SCRIPTURE

Read *Proverbs 12:12–26* to learn more about the rewards that await those who are honest.

**Truth Talk**   As a family, take time this week to talk about the following questions:

- How do you handle a situation in which being honest would hurt someone?
- When is it right to tell on someone, and when is it wrong?
- How can you help one another live in truth?

**GO online** www.osvcurriculum.com
For weekly scripture readings and seasonal resources

# People of Faith

**Joan of Arc** was true to God's will and truth. She had visions and heard voices that told her to lead an army to fight for truth and save France from invaders. She bravely told the truth about her visions and voices and saved France in many battles. However, Joan was accused of being against the Church and of being a witch. She was burned at the stake when she was still a teenager. Joan was named a saint in 1920, and her feast day is May 30.

▲ Saint Joan of Arc
1412–1431

 **Family Prayer**

Saint Joan of Arc, pray for us that we may grow strong in our faith and have the courage to speak and live the truth. Amen.

*In Unit 5 your child is learning about MORALITY.*

**CCC** *See Catechism of the Catholic Church 1741, 2465–2470 for further reading on chapter content.*

# Faith in Action!
## CATHOLIC SOCIAL TEACHING

In this unit, you learned that God asks Christians to live in peace and unity with all people. This is an important part of his plan for humans. Jesus has given you an example of how you are to treat others with care and kindness. When you act as a peacemaker and loving neighbor, you help make the world the way God intended it to be.

## Solidarity

When you look at the word *solidarity,* you can see the word *solid.* To stand in solidarity with others means to stand strong, or solid, next to them, helping them with their problems and sharing their joys. United, both groups of people become brothers and sisters in the one family of God.

## The Call to Unity

Sometimes it may be difficult to see God's plan for solidarity and unity. Countries fight one another in wars. Family members argue. Even friends sometimes walk away angry. But Christians are called to look for ways to grow in unity and peace. Bringing people together to solve problems is one way.

❓ **How can you help your family live in unity?**

❓ **How can you help the world live in solidarity?**

# Sisters in Spirit

Having a sister parish is a big responsibility and a great blessing. The adopting parish promises to help its sister parish. In turn, the adopted parish promises to help its new friends. The parishes of St. Ignatius Catholic Church in California and San Antonio Parish in El Salvador have adopted each other and become sister parishes.

God calls people to help one another in times of need. Let's see how one parish found a way to help another.

## Sisters in Action

When an earthquake struck El Salvador, many homes were damaged or destroyed. Men, women, teens, and children were needed to help rebuild. A group of parishioners from St. Ignatius traveled to El Salvador. Their friends at San Antonio Parish welcomed them warmly.

The parishioners of San Antonio were busy rebuilding their homes. Every family member, even children, helped make new bricks from mud. The people showed their friends from California how to make and bake the bricks.

The parishioners of St. Ignatius stood in solidarity by helping their sister parishioners build homes. San Antonio parishioners stood in solidarity by sharing their homes and hearts with the St. Ignatius parishioners. The parishes are now one family in spirit, friendship, and faith.

❓ What did the people of each parish learn from their sister parish?

# Reach Out!

## Reflect

Building a house is hard work. It takes lots of time, many people, and special tools. Building solidarity can be hard work, too. Many people must work together to build solidarity, and they need to have the right tools.

Tell how each of these "tools" could help people build solidarity.

teaching _____

_____

learning _____

_____

listening _____

_____

talking _____

_____

praying _____

_____

helping _____

_____

receiving help _____

_____

## Reaching Out

**Work Together**   As a class, choose a group to which you would like to reach out in solidarity. It might be another class in your school, a class in another school, or a club or sports team that meets at your school. Invite this group to help you plan and carry out an event that both groups will work on and enjoy. Use your imagination, have fun, and work together to build solidarity!

**A** **Work with Words**   Use the clues to solve the puzzle.

**Across**

1. This commandment says: You shall not kill.

3. The intentional killing of an innocent person

5. This commandment says: You shall not bear false witness against your neighbor.

6. To do things or act in certain ways that are requested by those in authority

7. The virtue that helps people dress, talk, and act in appropriate ways

9. Action taken to repair the damage done through sin

**Down**

2. This commandment specifically addresses sons and daughters.

4. Continuing the cycle of anger and hatred

7. Someone who gives up his or her life to witness to the truth of the faith

8. Solemn promises that are made to or before God

**B Check Understanding** Circle the word that best completes the statement.

11. Alfred Nobel is the founder of the Nobel Prizes, including the (Peace/Faith) Prize.

12. Thomas More was killed for refusing to say that the king of England was the head of the Catholic Church. More believed that the (bishop/pope) was the true head of the Church.

13. God's plan for humans includes living (without/with) families.

14. All actions that support and protect life obey the (fifth/ninth) commandment.

15. When you are (truthful/sinful), you are living as a follower of Jesus.

**C Make Connections** Write a brief response to each question or statement.

16. List two ways that school helps you respect and take care of your body.

_____

_____

17. List two ways that you respect and take care of your body at home.

_____

_____

18. Why will breaking the eighth commandment eventually leave you feeling lonely?

_____

_____

19. Explain what you have learned about the family.

_____

_____

20. What have you learned about being a faithful follower of Christ?

_____

_____

# Unit 6
# Sacraments

## In this unit you will...

learn about the Paschal mystery and how it is celebrated in the seasons of the liturgical year and through the Sacraments. Christ instituted the Sacraments as signs of God's love and presence, and to give us grace. The Eucharist is the heart of the Church's life. The Sacraments of Healing are about conversion, forgiveness, and healing.

Chapter 16

Chapter 17

Chapter 18

## Faith in Action!

**Catholic Social Teaching Principle:
Call to Family, Community,
and Participation**

# Chapter 16 The Church Year

 **Let Us Pray**

**Leader:** Creator God, we rejoice in the beauty and variety of your creation.

"The heavens declare the glory of God;
the sky proclaims its builder's craft."

*Psalm 19:2*

**All:** Creator God, we rejoice in the beauty and variety of your creation. Amen.

## Activity — Let's Begin

● **The Life Cycle**  All living things follow a pattern. They come to life, they grow and develop, and finally they die. This pattern is called a life cycle. Every year as the seasons change, you see changes in the world around you. The change of seasons affects you, too.

Think of one seasonal change that happens where you live. Describe the change.

_____

_____

_____

● **Make a Poster**  Create a poster that shows the wonders of nature in each of the four seasons. Then write about your favorite season.

# The Cycle of Life

 **Focus** What is the Paschal mystery?

Your life is full of cycles and seasons. As you grow in faith, you will notice them more. A wise man once wrote a poem about the cycle of life. It is in the Bible.

 **SCRIPTURE** Ecclesiastes 3:1–8

## The Right Time

There is an appointed time for everything,
and a time for every affair under the heavens.

A time to be born, and a time to die;
 a time to plant, and a time to uproot the plant.

A time to kill, and a time to heal;
 a time to tear down, and a time to build.

A time to weep, and a time to laugh;
 a time to mourn, and a time to dance.

A time to scatter stones, and a time to
  gather them;
 a time to embrace, and a time to be far
  from embraces.

A time to seek, and a time to lose;
 a time to keep, and a time to cast away.

A time to rend, and a time to sew;
 a time to be silent, and a time
  to speak.

A time to love, and a time to hate;
 a time of war, and a time of peace.

*Ecclesiastes 3:1–8*

❓ **What do you think the poet wants
you to understand?**

## The Paschal Mystery

Jesus experienced the natural cycle of life, but his life cycle did not end with his death on the cross. God the Father raised Jesus from the dead. Then Jesus ascended to join his Father in heaven. The suffering, death, Resurrection, and Ascension of Jesus are called the **Paschal mystery**. This mystery reveals that Jesus saved all humans from the power of sin and everlasting death.

The Church celebrates this mystery in every Sacrament and especially at every Eucharist. Every Sunday you gather with the parish community to celebrate the new life that Jesus' Resurrection gives you.

## Words of Faith

The **Paschal mystery** is the mystery of Jesus' suffering, death, Resurrection, and Ascension.

The **liturgical year** is the cycle of feasts and seasons that make up the Church's year of worship.

## The Liturgical Year

From week to week at Sunday Mass, you may notice different readings, hymns, and colors. These mark the seasons of the Church's year, called the **liturgical year**. The liturgical year begins on the first Sunday of Advent, usually around December 1, and ends with the feast of Christ the King.

**? What signs of the present liturgical season do you see?**

## Activity — Share Your Faith

**Reflect:** Reflect on the things you did last week.

**Share:** With a partner, share some of the best times and worst times you had last week.

**Act:** In the boxes below, sketch a symbol for the "times" of your life. If Monday was a happy time, draw a symbol to show that you were happy. Use different symbols to represent your "times."

| SUNDAY | MONDAY | TUESDAY | WEDNESDAY | THURSDAY | FRIDAY | SATURDAY |
|--------|--------|---------|-----------|----------|--------|----------|
|        |        |         |           |          |        |          |

# The Seasons

 **Focus** What are the seasons of the Church year?

Just as the seasons of the year mark the cycles of life and death in nature, the seasons of the liturgical year mark and celebrate the events of the Paschal mystery.

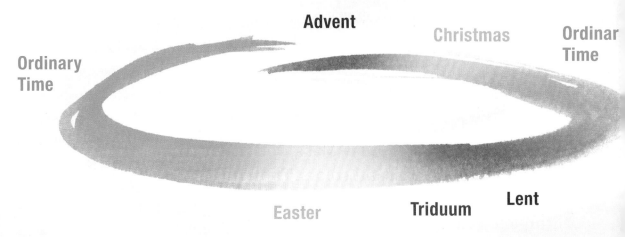

## Advent

Advent is the beginning of the Church year. The four weeks before Christmas are a time of preparation for the coming of Jesus. The Church asks the Holy Spirit to help people welcome Jesus into their hearts every day. The seasonal color is violet, a sign of waiting.

## Christmas

The Christmas Season lasts from Christmas Eve through the Sunday after Epiphany, which is twelve days after Christmas. It is a time to be joyful and to thank God the Father for sending his Son to become one of us. White and gold colors are reminders to celebrate the gift of Jesus.

❓ **How do your family and parish prepare for Christmas?**

# Lent

Lent lasts for forty days. It begins on Ash Wednesday and ends on Holy Thursday. Lent is a time to prepare for Easter by following Jesus more closely. The seasonal color of violet is used as a sign of penance.

# Triduum

The Easter Season is preceded by a three-day celebration of the Paschal mystery called the **Triduum**. It starts with the celebration of the Lord's Supper on Holy Thursday and ends with evening prayer on Easter Sunday.

# Easter

The Easter Season continues for fifty days until Pentecost. It is a time to remember your Baptism and to give thanks for the Resurrection of Jesus that saved all people from the power of sin and everlasting death. White or gold colors are used during this season as a sign of great joy.

# Ordinary Time

Ordinary Time is a season in two parts. The first is between the Christmas Season and the First Sunday of Lent. The second is between the Easter Season and Advent. Ordinary Time is the time to remember the works of Jesus and listen to his teachings. The color green is used during this season as a sign of hope and growth.

❓ **What is your favorite liturgical season?**

**W🕀rds of Faith**

**Triduum** is a celebration of the passion, death, and Resurrection of Christ. In the Church year, the Triduum begins on Holy Thursday evening and concludes on Easter Sunday night.

**Activity** — Connect Your Faith

**Remember His Love**   On the chart of seasons on the opposite page, design symbols to illustrate the saving actions of Jesus that are celebrated in each Church season.

# Living the Seasons

 **Focus** How do you celebrate the seasons of the Church year?

The seasons in nature affect the way you think and act. For example, you would not try to go ice fishing in the middle of summer. The Church also wants you to think and act according to its seasons.

## Seasons of the Heart

Each season of the Church gives you a different way to look at Jesus and the people and the world around you. Here are some ideas for ways to pray and live according to the seasons each year.

**Easter**
Celebrate the wonderful news that you have been saved. Share your experiences of how God has worked in your life.

**Advent**
Prepare for Jesus' coming into your heart by practicing patience.

**Lent**
Pray, fast, and focus your attention upon acts of penance. These actions will prepare you to celebrate Easter.

**Christmas**
Celebrate Jesus' birth by looking for the love of Jesus in everyone you meet.

**Ordinary Time**
Learn more about Jesus by reading the Bible. Imitate his love for those who are poor, suffering, or sick.

❓ **In what other ways can you celebrate the Church seasons?**

# Live Your Faith

**Describe the Church Seasons**   In the space below, draw scenes or symbols that make you think of a Church season. When possible, try to use the Church's colors for that season.

# Prayer of Praise

 Let Us Pray

*Gather and begin with the Sign of the Cross.*

*Sing together the refrain.*

Shout for joy, joy, joy! Shout for joy, joy, joy!
God is love, God is light, God is everlasting!

"Shout for Joy" © 1982, Jubilate Hymns, Ltd.

**Leader:** God, our good Father, you sent Jesus, your Son, to rescue us from the power of sin and everlasting death. This is our song.

**All:** *Sing refrain.*

**Leader:** Jesus, you came into this world of darkness as the light. Your words of love touched those who were sick and weak. You forgave sinners and freed them from shame. This is our song.

**All:** *Sing refrain.*

**Leader:** Jesus, you died on the cross, a sacrifice of love to set us free from our sins. This is our song.

**All:** *Sing refrain.*

**Leader:** Jesus, you were raised from the dead and ascended into heaven. You sent the Spirit to be with us always. We hope to share eternal life with you. This is our song.

**All:** *Sing refrain.*

**Leader:** Let us pray.

*Bow your heads as the leader prays.*

**All:** **Amen.**

**A** **Work with Words** Match each description in Column 1 with the correct term in Column 2.

**Column 1**

_____ **1.** a time of penance

_____ **2.** celebrates the birth of Jesus

_____ **3.** focuses on the Resurrection of Jesus

_____ **4.** prepares for the coming of Jesus

_____ **5.** focuses on Jesus' work and teachings

**Column 2**

**a.** Advent

**b.** Christmas

**c.** Ordinary Time

**d.** Lent

**e.** Easter

**B** **Check Understanding** Complete each statement with the correct term from the Word Bank.

**6.** The _____ mystery is the mystery of Jesus' suffering, death, Resurrection, and Ascension.

**7.** The _____ year is the cycle of feasts and seasons that make up the Church's year of worship.

**8.** _____ is a celebration of the Passion, death, and Resurrection of Christ.

**9.** In the Church year, the Triduum begins on Holy _____ evening and concludes on Easter Sunday night.

**10.** Ordinary Time is the time to remember the _____ of Jesus and listen to his teachings.

**WORD BANK**

liturgical
works
Paschal
Triduum
Thursday

# Family Faith

## Catholics Believe

- The Church year celebrates the Paschal mystery.
- The seasons of the liturgical year include Advent, Christmas, Lent, Easter, and Ordinary Time.

### ✝ SCRIPTURE

Read *Psalm 148:1–14* to praise the beauty of God's many wonderful creations.

**GO online** www.osvcurriculum.com
For weekly scripture readings and seasonal resources

## Activity

# Live Your Faith

**Notice Signs of the Season** Take a family walk or hike to look for signs of the season. Listen to the sounds, look for changes, and take in the beauty of God's creation. Discuss how these signs of the season in nature reflect the liturgical season as well. Pray a simple prayer of thanks as you list each sign of the season. Then celebrate with a snack or meal.

# People of Faith

**Bede** was born in Sunderland, England. After he became a monk, Bede studied the Scriptures. He wrote many lessons about the Bible and explained ways to reform the Church. Bede also became an expert in the history of the English Church. When he realized that he was dying, Bede worked hard and finished translating the Gospel of John into English. The feast day of Saint Bede is May 25.

▲ Saint Bede
673–735

## 🙌 Family Prayer

O God, help us grow closer to you by our worship at the Eucharist, our learning of our Catholic faith, and our devotion to prayer. Amen.

---

# Chapter 17 — The Seven Sacraments

## Let Us Pray

**Leader:** Lord, we see your mightiness in the works you have done.

"May the glory of the LORD endure forever; may the LORD be glad in these works!"

*Psalm 104:31*

**All:** Lord, we see your mightiness in the works you have done. Amen.

### Activity — Let's Begin

**I Will Remember**   Juana's favorite time of year is spring. Every spring Juana and her *abuela,* or grandmother, would garden together. This spring was different. Abuela had died during the winter, and Juana missed her very much.

One day Juana walked past the flower bed and noticed buds on the green shoots. "Those are the flowers from the bulbs Abuela and I planted in the fall!" she thought. "When I see them, I will remember that she is living with God now."

What things remind you of special people in your life when they are not with you?

• Why is it important to remember these people?

_____

_____

• **Make Reminder Cards**   Make reminder cards to send to three people who are special to you.

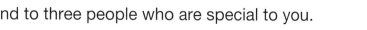

**231**

# God's Love Is Present

 **Focus** What is a Sacrament?

The flowers in Juana's garden were signs to her that her *abuela* still lived with God and was loved by him. God the Father sent Jesus into the world as a sign of his love for all people. He pointed the way to God for all who followed him.

Jesus welcomed people like Peter and Zacchaeus, and they changed their lives for him. Jesus showed people God the Father's forgiveness. He healed some and called others to serve God's people. Through Jesus' words and actions, many people experienced God's saving love. Jesus made God and his love present.

Jesus said this to his Apostles at the Last Supper.

### SCRIPTURE

No one comes to the Father except through me. If you know me, then you will also know my Father. From now on you do know him and have seen him.

*John 14:6–7*

It was only after Jesus' Resurrection that his Apostles began to understand who Jesus really was. Gradually, they came to understand that he was not just a sign of God—he really was God!

**❓ How did Jesus show God's saving love to the world?**

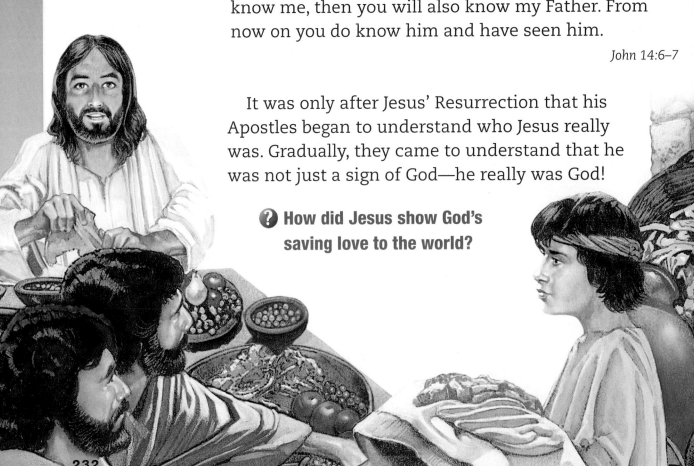

# Signs of God's Love

Jesus told his followers that he would always be with them and that they would continue his saving work. One of the ways that Jesus is with his people today is through the seven **Sacraments**. The Sacraments are actions of the Holy Spirit at work in Christ's Body, the Church. Jesus is present in the Sacraments.

The Church has named seven Sacraments that have their origins in Jesus. Each one celebrates a way that Jesus' saving work continues in the world.

## The Seven Sacraments

| | |
|---|---|
| Baptism | New life in Christ |
| Confirmation | Strengthening through the Holy Spirit |
| Eucharist | Unity and salvation in Christ through the Body and Blood of Christ |
| Reconciliation | Conversion and forgiveness through Christ |
| Anointing of the Sick | Healing in Christ |
| Holy Orders | Ministry to Christ's Body, the Church |
| Matrimony | Marriage covenant as a sign of Christ's covenant with his Church |

## Activity — Share Your Faith

**Reflect:** Think of someone you love.

**Share:** Sketch a sign that reminds you of the person. Explain the sign to the class as you say the name.

**Act:** With your classmates, play a game matching the signs and names.

# Eucharist

 **Focus** What is the heart of the Christian life?

Jesus often ate meals with his friends. On the night before he died, Jesus shared a meal with his Apostles and asked them to remember him always.

## ✝ SCRIPTURE                                    Luke 22:17–20

## The Last Supper

Then [Jesus] took a cup, gave thanks, and said, "Take this and share it among yourselves; for I tell you [that] from this time on I shall not drink of the fruit of the vine until the kingdom of God comes." Then he took the bread, said the blessing, broke it, and gave it to them, saying, "This is my body, which will be given for you; do this in memory of me." And likewise the cup after they had eaten, saying, "This cup is the new covenant in my blood, which will be shed for you."

*Luke 22:17–20*

### Breaking of the Bread

After Jesus was raised from the dead and returned to the Father, his followers gathered weekly for a special meal. They called this meal the "breaking of the bread." They believed, as Catholics do today, that Jesus was present when they broke bread together. Today this meal is called the **Eucharist**, or Mass.

❓ **When did you first receive Jesus in Holy Communion? Tell what you remember about the day.**

## The Eucharist

The word *Eucharist* means "thanksgiving." At the beginning of Mass, you ask God's mercy because of your sins. Your venial sins can be forgiven through your celebration of the Eucharist. You listen to God's word. You thank God the Father for the great gift of his Son. When you receive Jesus in Holy Communion, you are united with the other members of the Body of Christ.

## Living the Eucharist

When Jesus told the Apostles to "do this in memory of me," he did not mean only that they should break bread together. He meant that they should live their lives as he did. Living the Eucharist means loving, welcoming, and forgiving others. You live the Eucharist when you share with those who do not have what you do.

❓ **What are some ways that you can live the Eucharist?**

**Words of Faith**

**Eucharist** is the Sacrament through which Catholics are united with the life, death, and Resurrection of Jesus.

### Activity — Connect Your Faith

**Dinner Guests**    Think of people you would like to have as company for dinner at your house, and write their names on the chairs. In the space on the table, write what you might do to welcome them and show them the love of Jesus.

# Participating at Mass

 **Focus** How can you participate actively in Mass?

Do you go to Mass, or do you participate in Mass? Do you know the difference? If you arrive at church on Sunday, slink into the pew, and daydream for the next hour, you are only *going* to Mass.

Mass is an excellent time for you to take an active role in building your relationship with God. It is your chance to join with the rest of your parish in lifting your voices and souls in praise of God.

## Take Part

- Join in singing the hymns and responses.

- Listen to the word of God as it is proclaimed in the Scriptures and the homily.

- Pray with the priest as he says the Eucharistic Prayer. Think about the meaning of the words, especially those Jesus used at the Last Supper.

- Offer a greeting of peace to the people around you.

- Open your heart to Jesus and the Church as you receive Holy Communion.

- Think of one way to live the Eucharist during the following week.

❓ **Why is it important to participate actively in Mass?**

# Live Your Faith

**Prepare a Liturgy**   Prepare a liturgy for your school. Your teacher will help you by sharing the Scripture readings for the day. Listen as your teacher reads these passages to you, and think about what they say. Choose songs that relate to the readings. Write one prayer of the faithful.

Date _____

Scripture _____

_____

_____

Songs _____

_____

_____

Prayer of the Faithful _____

_____

_____

_____

_____

_____

# Prayer of Thanks

 **Let Us Pray**

*Gather and begin with the Sign of the Cross.*

Reader: The Lord be with you.

All: **And with your spirit.**

Reader: Lift up your hearts.

All: **We lift them up to the Lord.**

Reader: Let us give thanks to the Lord our God.

All: **It is right and just.**

*Sing together.*

We come to share our story,
   we come to break the bread,
We come to know our rising from the dead.

"Song of the Body of Christ" © 2001, GIA Publications, Inc.

Reader: Because you love us, you gave us this great and beautiful world.

All: *Sing refrain.*

Reader: Because you love us, you sent Jesus your Son to bring us to you.

All: *Sing refrain.*

Leader: Let us pray.

*Bow your heads as the leader prays.*

All: **Amen.**

**A** **Work with Words**   Fill in the circle next to the answer that best completes each statement.

1. There are _____ Sacraments.

   ○ seven                    ○ eight                    ○ nine

2. _____ is present in all of the Sacraments.

   ○ Water                    ○ Jesus                    ○ The Bible

3. The early Christians _____ the Eucharist.

   ○ celebrated               ○ did not celebrate   ○ invented

4. Eucharist means "_____."

   ○ morality                 ○ heaven                   ○ thanksgiving

5. When you _____, you continue Jesus' work in the world.

   ○ go to religion class   ○ sing hymns           ○ live the Eucharist

**B** **Check Understanding**   Complete each sentence by circling the correct answer.

6. After Jesus' Resurrection, the Apostles began to understand that (he was God/he was gone forever).

7. The Sacraments are actions of the (priest/Holy Spirit) at work in Christ's Body, the Church.

8. When you receive Jesus in Holy Communion, you (forgive/are united with) the other members of the Body of Christ.

**C** **Make Connections**

9. What are some ways you can live the Eucharist?

   _____

   _____

10. What are some ways you can participate actively in the Mass?

   _____

   _____

# Family Faith

## Catholics Believe

- The seven Sacraments are signs, instituted by Christ, that give grace.

- The Sacrament of the Eucharist is at the heart of Christian life.

### ✝ SCRIPTURE

Read *Psalm 107* as a way to give thanks to God for his blessings.

**GO online** www.osvcurriculum.com
For weekly scripture readings and seasonal resources

## Activity
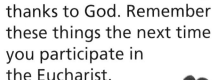
# Live Your Faith

**Create a Thank-you List** In the Eucharistic Prayer you hear the words "Lift up your hearts" and "Let us give thanks to the Lord our God." Make a list of things for which you offer thanks to God. Remember these things the next time you participate in the Eucharist.

# People of Faith

**Margaret Mary Alacoque** was born into a peasant family in France. When she joined a convent, Margaret Mary developed a deep prayer life. She had several visions in which Jesus told her about his loving heart. Devotion to the Sacred Heart of Jesus, which includes participating in Mass and receiving the Eucharist on the first Friday of each month, developed and grew in the Church because of her inspiration. Her feast day is October 16.

▲ Saint Margaret
Mary Alacoque
1647–1690

##  Family Prayer

Saint Margaret Mary Alacoque, pray for us that we may deepen our prayer lives and our devotion to the Eucharist. Amen.

# Chapter 18 Healing and Reconciliation

*Invite*

## Let Us Pray

**Leader:** Merciful God, be always with us as we pray.

"Remember your compassion and love,
O Lord;
for they are ages old."

*Psalm 25:6*

**All:** Merciful God, be always with us as we pray. Amen.

### Activity
## Let's Begin

**Forgiveness**   Complete these sentences.

• Forgiveness is easy when . . . _____

_____

• Forgiveness is difficult when . . . _____

_____

• I can always forgive . . . _____

_____

Now think about times when you have forgiven someone or been forgiven by someone.

• When I forgive, I . . . _____

_____

• When I am forgiven, I . . . _____

_____

**Write About Forgiveness**   Write a story about a time when you forgave someone, or when someone forgave you.

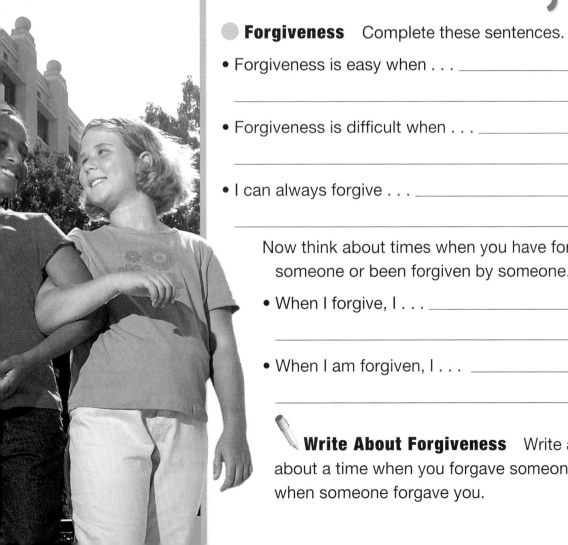

**241**

# God's Forgiveness

◎ **Focus** Who is forgiven?

Jesus showed God's forgiveness to others through his words and actions. In this story, Jesus meets a wealthy tax collector who decides to become his follower.

✝ **SCRIPTURE**                                              Luke 19:1–10

## The Story of Zacchaeus

One day Jesus was passing through the town of Jericho. Zacchaeus, a rich tax collector, wanted to see Jesus and learn about him. Zacchaeus was short, so he climbed a tree to see past the crowd.

Jesus noticed Zacchaeus in the tree. He said, "Zacchaeus, come down quickly, for today I must stay at your house." Zacchaeus came down happily.

The crowd complained, saying that Jesus should not stay with Zacchaeus because Zacchaeus was a sinner.

Zacchaeus told Jesus that he would give money to those who were poor. He offered to give anyone he had cheated four times the amount of money that he owed to that person.

"Today salvation has come to this house," said Jesus. "For the Son of Man has come to seek and to save what was lost."

Based on *Luke 19:1–10*

❓ **Who has taught you the most about forgiveness? What did the person or persons say or do?**

242

# Turn to God

God is always ready and waiting to forgive. When you decide to turn away from sin and turn back toward God, you are experiencing conversion. God welcomes you back, just as Jesus welcomed Zacchaeus.

During his life Jesus forgave many people in his Father's name. After his Resurrection, Jesus told his disciples that he would send the Holy Spirit, who would give them the power to forgive sins. Today the Church continues to celebrate God's forgiveness in the **Sacrament of Reconciliation**. Sometimes this is called Penance or Confession. In this Sacrament, you receive God's forgiveness of sins through the Church. The grace of this Sacrament strengthens you to make peace with those whom you may have hurt.

## Words of Faith

The **Sacrament of Reconciliation** celebrates God's mercy and forgiveness and a sinner's reconciliation with God and with the Church through the absolution of the priest.

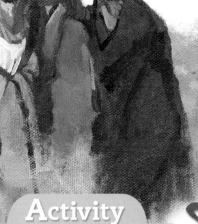

## Activity — Share Your Faith

**Reflect:** Think of someone who has forgiven you. Why did you need forgiveness?

**Share:** In groups discuss ways to show you are sorry and make peace with others.

**Act:** List two ways that you can be more forgiving of others.

_____

_____

# The Sacraments of Healing

 **Focus** How does the Church celebrate forgiveness and healing?

Celebrating the Sacrament of Reconciliation is a public sign that you are willing to turn away from sin and toward the love of God and the community. When you confess your sins to a priest, you ask for God's forgiveness through the power the Holy Spirit gives to the Church. God will forgive all sins, even mortal sins, if you are truly sorry and want to change your heart. When the priest says the words of **absolution**, you know that God has taken your sins away.

❓ **Why is it important to celebrate the Sacrament of Reconciliation?**

## Repairing the Harm

God forgives your sins, but the effects of your sins are still in the world. You must do what you can to repair the harm your sin has caused. Part of making up for your sin is to do the **penance** that the priest gives you.

## God's Healing Love

Today the Church anoints the sick or dying through the **Sacrament of the Anointing of the Sick**. This Sacrament strengthens those who celebrate it and reminds them of God's healing love. God's love and forgiveness are available to all who turn to him.

In Jesus' time, people thought that sickness was God's punishment for someone's sin. But Jesus taught a different message.

### ✝ SCRIPTURE — John 9:1–38

# The Man Born Blind

*O*ne day Jesus saw a man who had been blind from birth. His disciples asked him, "Why is this man blind? Is it because of his own sin or that of his parents?"

Jesus answered, "Neither he nor his parents sinned; it is so that the works of God might be made more visible through him."

Jesus rubbed clay on the man's eyes and told him to go to a certain place and wash it off. When the man did, he could see!

Many did not believe that Jesus had done this. When the man came back, Jesus asked the man, "Do you believe in the Son of Man? . . . You have seen him and the one speaking with you is he."

The man answered, "I do believe, Lord."

Based on *John 9:1–38*

# Words of Faith

Words of **absolution** are spoken by the priest during the Sacrament of Reconciliation.

**Penance** is the name for the prayer, offering, or good works the priest gives you in the Sacrament of Reconciliation.

The **Sacrament of the Anointing of the Sick** brings Jesus' healing touch to strengthen, comfort, and forgive the sins of those who are seriously ill or close to death.

## Activity — Connect Your Faith

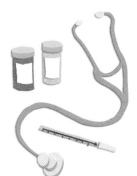

**Think About Healing** In the space below, name an illness that you've had or that someone you know has had. Then add the people and medicines or other things God has provided for healing.

_____

_____

245

# Prepare for Reconciliation

 **Focus** How can you prepare to receive God's forgiveness?

You may feel uncomfortable about telling your sins to a priest. Remember that the priest is not there to scare or punish you. He is acting as a servant of God. He will know your sorrow and grant you God's forgiveness.

Are you wondering how you will know what to say? Here are some suggestions to help you prepare to celebrate the Sacrament of Reconciliation.

## Before You Go

### Examine your conscience
Try to remember as best you can the sins you have committed. Look at the Ten Commandments, the Beatitudes, and the laws of the Church. Ask yourself whether you have followed these laws and guides.

### Pray to the Holy Spirit
Ask for guidance in discovering your weaknesses.

### Select a Scripture passage
Choose one that inspires you to turn away from sin and make a fresh start.

### Make up your mind to do penance
This is a way of healing any hurts or harm you may have caused through your sins.

### Show your sorrow
Pray the Act of Contrition.

### Decide to avoid sin
Resolve that with the help and guidance of the Holy Spirit, you will resist temptation and do better.

❓ **How do you feel after you celebrate the Sacrament of Penance and Reconciliation?**

Activity

# Live Your Faith

**Write a Skit** Write a skit about helping someone learn how to prepare for the Sacrament of Reconciliation.

Title: ______________________________

Characters: ______________, ______________

______________________________

______________________________

______________________________

Plot: ______________________________

______________________________

______________________________

______________________________

______________________________

______________________________

______________________________

______________________________

______________________________

______________________________

______________________________

______________________________

______________________________

______________________________

______________________________

# Prayer for Peace

 **Let Us Pray**

*Gather and begin with the Sign of the Cross.*

**Reader 1:** Merciful Father, we are together on earth, alone in the universe.

**All:** **Grant us peace, Lord.**

**Reader 2:** Look at us and help us love one another. Teach us to understand one another, just as you understand us.

**All:** **Grant us peace, Lord.**

**Reader 3:** Make our souls as fresh as the morning. Make our hearts as innocent as a baby's.

**All:** **Grant us peace, Lord.**

**Reader 4:** May we forgive one another and forget the past. And may we have peace within—and in our world today and forever.

**All:** **Grant us peace, Lord.**

**Leader:** Let us pray.

*Bow your heads as the leader prays.*

**All:** **Amen.**

*Sing together.*

Go now in peace.
Go now in peace.
May the love of God
surround you ev'rywhere,
ev'rywhere you may go.

"Go Now in Peace" ©1976 Hinshaw Music, Inc.

**Check Understanding**   Solve the crossword puzzle.

### Down

1. welcoming someone back after a wrong has been done
2. These separate you from God and others.
3. This is done for those who are very sick or dying.
4. God's love is available to all who _____ to him.
6. When you tell the priest your sins, you are really _____ to God.

### Across

5. the Sacrament that celebrates God's forgiveness of sins
7. When the priest gives this, you know that God has taken your sins away.
8. deciding to turn away from sin and turn back to God
9. This helps you make up for your sins.
10. another name for Reconciliation

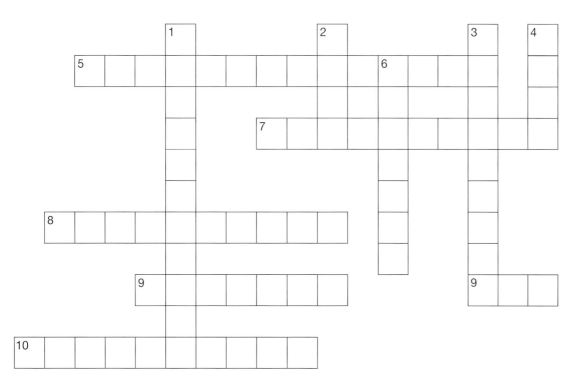

# Family Faith

## Catholics Believe

- God's forgiveness is offered to all who seek it.

- The Sacraments of Reconciliation and the Anointing of the Sick celebrate God's healing love.

### SCRIPTURE

Read *Matthew 18:21–35* to learn from Jesus how we should forgive.

**www.osvcurriculum.com**
For weekly scripture readings and seasonal resources

## Activity
# Live Your Faith

**Play the Yarn Game** Gather your family in a circle with a ball of yarn. Hold the end of the yarn in one hand and the ball in the other. Hold your end of the yarn and toss the ball to another person. Tell that person you are sorry for something that you did to him or her. Then that person repeats the action with someone else. Repeat the process until you weave a web of forgiveness with the yarn. Pray the Act of Contrition together.

# People of Faith

**Matt Talbot** was born in Dublin, Ireland, to a family that was poor. As he grew up he developed a drinking problem. After years of heavy drinking, Matt decided to become sober. He had hurt and disappointed many of his friends and family members, but he asked their forgiveness. He prayed and practiced self-sacrifice. Matt gave most of his lumberyard wages to people who were poor or hungry. He made a better life for himself and many other people.

▲ Venerable Matt Talbot 1856–1925

## Family Prayer

O God, give us the grace to overcome our shortcomings, and teach us to be self-sacrificing, as Matt Talbot was. Amen.

*In Unit 6 your child is learning about SACRAMENTS.*

DISCOVER

Catholic Social
Teaching:

Call to Family,
Community, and
Participation

# Faith in Action!
## CATHOLIC SOCIAL TEACHING

In this unit, you have learned that God made people to live together in families and in communities. He has given humans the gift of other people to share good times and troubles. People make the best use of this gift by working together to create happy and peaceful communities.

## Call to Community

Humans were not created to live alone and apart from one another. God made people to live with and for others. Humans belong to one another because God is Father of all, and Jesus is everyone's brother and Savior.

A community is a group of people who share common beliefs and activities. The first community you belong to is your family. You belong to the Church community through Baptism. You also belong to other communities, such as neighborhoods, towns or cities, and the world. Baptized Christians have a responsibility to participate in all of these communities.

❓ **How might you and your classmates take more responsibility for your school community?**

❓ **What are you willing to do to help others in the neighborhood or world community live better lives?**

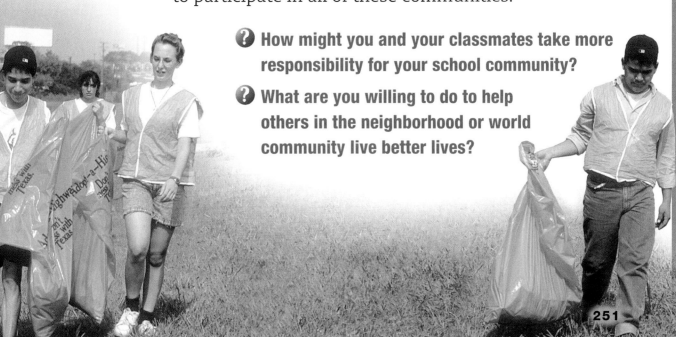

# Neighborhood Problems

**G**od's love is revealed in families and communities. Let's see how one community joined together to make their city better.

**C**rime and drugs were entering Connecticut. Children attending a local middle school were no longer safe coming to school. The neighborhood was falling apart. Something had to be done.

"But what could one person do?" a resident asked himself. Alone, he could do little. But together with his neighbors, he could do great things. The man and his neighbors, who belong to St. Rose of Lima parish, knew that they could work together to solve some of the community's problems.

## Neighborhood Solutions

Before long, other churches and organizations joined the effort. For more than ten years, ECCO, Elm City Congregations Organized, has done amazing things for local residents.

Working with the local police, members of ECCO have put drug pushers out of business. They have helped change the laws that allowed liquor stores near schools. Now children at Clemente Middle School can safely enjoy recess outside.

The group begun by the St. Rose of Lima parishioners has also made sure that clean and decent housing is available. Above all, the group members have learned the importance of working together to make a better community for everyone.

❓ **How did ECCO members show that they took responsibility for their community?**

# Reach Out!

## An Ideal Community

Use the diagram to design what you think an ideal neighborhood community would be like. The diagram represents the main street and two cross streets in a neighborhood.

Draw housing, schools, parks, and stores and other services that the community might need.

## Reaching Out

**Create a Neighborhood**   Together with your classmates, design a larger neighborhood. As a group, decide which features of your new neighborhood should be near other features. Then invite another class to "visit" your neighborhood. Ask your visitors to suggest any features that you might have forgotten.

253

# UNIT 6 REVIEW

**A** **Work with Words** Complete each sentence with the correct word. Then find the word in the word search.

```
k  c  b  l  y  e  c  n  a  n  e  p  o  q  r
i  z  y  w  g  n  n  s  t  m  n  w  r  c  a
t  e  s  a  c  r  a  m  e  n  t  s  d  n  e
e  e  k  n  d  i  m  h  o  t  l  r  i  n  y
f  u  z  o  r  e  s  j  l  o  g  t  n  k  l
o  c  b  a  n  o  i  n  t  i  n  g  a  i  a
p  h  u  n  c  z  o  l  e  i  e  w  r  c  c
k  a  q  i  z  i  f  i  j  r  m  h  y  d  i
y  r  e  t  s  y  m  l  a  h  c  s  a  p  g
b  i  z  n  n  x  y  k  s  v  s  r  d  g  r
m  s  z  g  f  a  d  t  w  b  r  k  a  n  u
z  t  n  i  x  m  u  u  d  i  r  t  h  p  t
k  k  z  f  o  r  g  i  v  e  n  e  s  s  i
x  a  w  e  o  x  s  i  b  j  k  e  f  g  l
k  n  o  i  t  a  i  l  i  c  n  o  c  e  r
```

1. The Sacrament of _____ strengthens you to make peace with those whom you may have hurt.

2. Absolution is spoken by a priest to communicate God's _____.

3. Jesus' healing touch strengthens and forgives the sins of those who are seriously ill in the Sacrament of the _____ of the Sick.

4. _____ is the Sacrament through which Christians are united with the life, death, and Resurrection of Jesus.

5. The cycle of the Church's feasts and seasons is the

   _____.

6. Through the _____ Jesus saves us from sin and death.

7. _____ is a prayer or action the priest gives you to help you make up for the effects of your sins.

8. The _____ are signs that give grace.

9. The _____ celebrates the Passion, death, and Resurrection of Christ.

10. _____ Time is a season of the Church year.

## B Check Understanding   Fill in the circle next to the best answer.

**11.** Early Christians honored Jesus with a special meal called "the breaking of the bread." Today this tradition is called _____.

  ○ the breaking of the bread        ○ a feast day
  ○ the Eucharist

**12.** Jesus showed that the most generous gift is to _____

  ○ spend all your money on presents
  ○ make your own greeting cards
  ○ give your life for others

**13.** Two of the seven Sacraments are _____.

  ○ Scripture and Tradition        ○ prayer and study
  ○ Baptism and Matrimony

**14.** The seasonal color for Advent and Lent is _____.

  ○ green        ○ violet        ○ red

**15.** The seasonal colors for _____ are white and gold.

  ○ Christmas and Easter        ○ Ordinary Time and Lent
  ○ Pentecost and Advent

## C Make Connections   Write responses on the lines below.

**16.** Name two different seasons of the Church year, and tell one way you can grow closer to God during each.

_____

**17.** Why is it important to participate actively in Mass?

_____

**18.** Name three things you can do to prepare for the Sacrament of Reconciliation.

_____

**19.** Why is it important to celebrate the Sacrament of Reconciliation?

_____

**20.** How do the Sacraments help you grow in faith?

_____

# Unit 7
# Kingdom of God

## In this unit you will...

learn that our mission is to promote the kingdom of God. We do this by proclaiming the gospel and being a sign of Christ to others. We are called to be generous stewards of our possessions and to work for the good of all people. How we live our lives now, matters. We try to live justly so that we can live forever with God in heaven.

Chapter 19

Chapter 20

Chapter 21

## Faith in Action!

**Catholic Social Teaching Principle:**
**Option for the Poor and Vulnerable**

# A Generous Spirit

## Let Us Pray

**Leader:** Kindly God, your generous spirit amazes all your children.
"How good God is to the upright, the LORD,
to those who are clean of heart!"

*Psalm 73:1*

**All:** Kindly God, your generous spirit amazes all your children.
Amen.

## Activity

## Let's Begin

**The Giveaway** Some Native Americans have a custom called *giveaway*. Instead of receiving gifts on his or her birthday, a person gives away a possession that someone else has admired during the year. Native Americans say that this custom helps them show gratitude for the gifts of life and good fortune.

• Think about something you own that someone else has admired. Explain how difficult it would it be for you to give that possession away. Why?

_____

_____

_____

**Write About Gifts** Make a list of the best gifts you have ever received and the best gifts you have ever given. Share the list with a partner.

# Desire for Riches

 **Focus** What does Jesus want you to know about riches?

Many cultures have stories that explore how much is too much. Here is one from ancient Greece.

### A STORY

## KING MIDAS

Long ago and far away there lived in Greece a king named Midas. One day an old man wandered into King Midas's rose garden. Midas had his servants feed and care for the man.

Midas escorted the old man back to his home. The god Bacchus was pleased with the care Midas had given the man. Bacchus granted Midas one wish. Midas wished that everything he touched would turn to gold. And his wish was granted!

When he reached his palace, Midas ordered a feast to celebrate his good fortune. But when Midas tried to eat, his food turned to gold when he touched it. Midas soon grew hungry and thirsty, and he complained to his daughter. But when Midas's daughter hugged her father to console him, she also turned to gold!

**?** **What can you learn from the story of Midas?**

## Poor in Spirit

King Midas did not think of the consequences of his wish. Because Midas put his desire for riches first, he hurt himself and others.

Everything that God made is good. People are good. The things that people create with love and care are good. But Jesus taught that possessions are not the most important things. Do you remember the story found in *Matthew 19:16–22* about the rich young man? Jesus loved him and wanted him to be happy.

❓ **What did Jesus tell the rich young man to do?**

## First Things First

Sometimes people need to leave behind their material possessions in order to have the time and energy to do good. The Apostles left their homes, families, and jobs in order to follow Jesus and help him spread God's word.

### Faith Fact

In the Bible, the word *blessed* means "favored with the blessings of God."

The first beatitude says, "Blessed are the poor in spirit, for theirs is the kingdom of heaven" (*Matthew 5:3*). Those who do not become too attached to their possessions are able to work for love and peace in the world and help bring about God's kingdom.

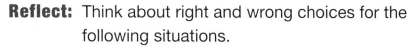

**Activity** Share Your Faith

**Reflect:** Think about right and wrong choices for the following situations.

- A video game that you want is on an outdoor table during a sidewalk sale.
- Someone else wins an award that you wanted.

**Share:** In a small group, role-play one of these situations, showing how you could make a good choice.

**Act:** Write what you would do to make a good choice in the other situation. Why would this be a good choice?

# Living a Generous Life

 **Focus** What do the seventh and tenth commandments teach you?

There are two commandments that help you have the right attitude about material possessions. The seventh commandment says this: You shall not steal. The tenth commandment says this: You shall not covet your neighbor's goods.

Theft, greed, and envy are all sins against the seventh and tenth commandments. Theft is taking what is not yours. When you have **envy**, you resent or are sad because someone else possesses something that you really want. Envy harms the Body of Christ because it divides God's people rather than bringing everyone together. **Greed** is the desire to gain earthly possessions without concern for what is reasonable or right.

## An Open Heart

Humility, a spirit of generosity, and trust in God's care can help overcome envy and greed. If you are happy with what you have received, then you can be happy for the good fortune of others. Caring too much for things usually brings unhappiness and disappointment.

Because everything comes from God, all people have a right to what they need to live comfortably. As a member of the Body of Christ, you are called to share your possessions with others, especially those who do not have food, shelter, or decent clothing.

❓ **In what ways are people your age tempted to be envious or greedy?**

## Called to Stewardship

The seventh and tenth commandments require you to be generous with others. Being generous means giving more than is necessary.

God created the world for all creatures and called humans to stewardship. As stewards, or caretakers, people are called to use natural resources well and protect the environment for everyone now and in the future; to respect all life as a gift from God; and to share time, money, and talent to help others.

### SCRIPTURE · Mark 12:41–44

## The Widow's Contribution

Jesus watched people put money into the temple treasury. Many rich people put in large sums of money. A poor widow put in two small coins worth only a few cents. Jesus said to his disciples, "I say to you, this poor widow put in more than all the others. They contributed their extra money, but the widow has given all she had."

Based on *Mark 12:41–44*

❓ **How did the widow contribute more than the rest?**

❓ **Who do you know who has a generous spirit?**

Activity — Connect Your Faith

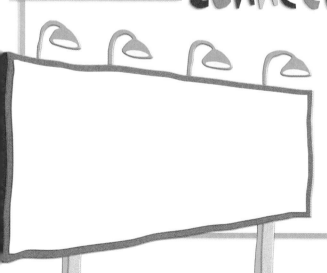

**Be a Good Steward** Sketch a design for a stewardship ad that shows you or your group giving your time, talent, or treasure for the good of others. Encourage other people in your parish to share in similar ways.

# Practice Generosity

 **Focus** How can you learn to have a more generous spirit?

God knew that it would be easier for you to help and care for one another if you did not let possessions get in the way. He gave you the seventh and tenth commandments to encourage good habits and help build a world of peace, love, and justice.

You have the ability to be as generous as God wants you to be. Here are some ideas that can help you be more generous every day.

### SHARE
If you have a book or CD that someone else would enjoy, lend it to that person. Perhaps he or she cannot afford to buy this item.

### DO NOT ENVY OTHERS; BE GLAD FOR WHAT THEY HAVE
When you see someone who has something you want, be glad for that person rather than being envious.

### SEPARATE NEEDS FROM WANTS
Before you ask for or buy something new, stop and think, "Do I really need that, or do I just want it?"

### LIVE SIMPLY
Reduce the clutter in your room. Look for things that you no longer use, and give them to the Saint Vincent de Paul Society, Goodwill Industries, or another local charity.

❓ **Why do people sometimes forget to be generous?**

# Live Your Faith

**Spread God's Word**   In the space below, design an ad that will remind people to be generous with one another. Use what you have learned in this chapter.

♥ Share ♥ Give ♥ Generous Spirit ♥ Love ♥

Love ♥ Generous Spirit ♥ Give ♥ Share

Share ♥ Give ♥ Generous Spirit ♥ Love

♥ Share ♥ Give ♥ Generous Spirit ♥ Love ♥

# Prayer for Help

 **Let Us Pray**

*Gather and begin with the Sign of the Cross.*

**Leader:** God our Father, please hear our prayer. Help us see your Son in others.

**All:** **So that we may give freely and generously.**

**Reader 1:** Help us appreciate what we have been given.

**All:** **So that we may show gratitude to those who have been generous to us.**

**Reader 2:** Help us be happy when others have received gifts.

**All:** **So that we may be good friends to them.**

**Reader 3:** Help us remember others.

**All:** **So that we are willing to share our possessions.**

**Leader:** We ask for your guidance and continued love in Jesus' name by the grace of the Holy Spirit.

**All:** **Amen.**

*Sing together.*

For your gracious
blessing, for your
wondrous word, for
your loving kindness,
we give thanks, O God.

"For Your Gracious Blessing," Traditional.

**A** **Work with Words**   Fill in the circle next to the answer that best completes each statement.

1. The _____ commandment states that you should not steal.

    ○ sixth          ○ seventh        ○ eighth

2. The responsibility to care for all of God's creation is _____.

    ○ stewardship    ○ conscience     ○ generosity

3. The _____ commandment states that you should not desire what others have.

    ○ eighth         ○ ninth          ○ tenth

4. _____ is being sad or resentful when someone else possesses something you want.

    ○ Stealing       ○ Generosity     ○ Envy

5. _____ is the unlimited gathering of material possessions.

    ○ Greed          ○ Generosity     ○ Stewardship

**B** **Check Understanding**   Below are examples of how you can keep the seventh and tenth commandments. On the space provided, write the number of the commandment that the example refers to.

6. _____ Donating your outgrown clothing to charity

7. _____ Finding a toy in the parking lot of a store, and turning it in to the lost and found

8. _____ Sharing your possessions with a brother or sister

9. _____ Not eating food in a grocery store until after you have paid for it

10. _____ Being thankful for what you have

**265**

## Catholics Believe

- The commandments call you to be generous and to have the right attitude toward possessions.

- The goods of the earth are meant for the benefit of the whole human family.

### SCRIPTURE

Read *2 Corinthians 9:6–9* to find out how the Corinthians were challenged to be generous.

**GO online** **www.osvcurriculum.com**
For weekly scripture readings and seasonal resources

## Activity

# Live Your Faith

**Start a New Custom** Talk about the *giveaway* story at the beginning of this chapter.

- How hard would it be to add this custom to a birthday or to another celebration?
- In what other ways could you express a generous spirit toward others?

Choose one way, and decide how you will act on it as a family.

▲ Catherine de Hueck Doherty 1900–1985

# People of Faith

**Catherine de Hueck Doherty** was a Russian noblewoman who moved to Canada. She saw poverty in the world around her and decided to act. She founded the first Friendship House, a welcoming place for those who are poor. She then started Madonna House, a farm that combines prayer and a simple lifestyle. Since her death in 1985, Madonna Houses and Friendship Houses have continued to spread in the United States and Canada.

 ## Family Prayer

Jesus, help us imitate Catherine de Hueck Doherty's caring spirit as we learn how to share what we have with those in need. Amen.

# Chapter 20 The Church in the World

 **Let Us Pray**

**Leader:** Giving God, thank you for the world you made and all the people who share it.

"How good it is, how pleasant,
    where the people dwell as one!"

*Psalm 133:1*

**All:** Giving God, thank you for the world you made and all the people who share it. Amen.

 **Activity** — **Let's Begin**

● **Different, Yet the Same** Look around you. You are surrounded by differences. The people sitting in the room with you have different hairstyles, different eye colors, and different skin tones. They have different last names and may have different cultural backgrounds.

   And yet, with all of these differences, you all belong to the same human family.

Look at the person next to you. What things about the two of you are alike and what things are different?

_____

Which are more important: the things that are alike or the things that are different?

_____

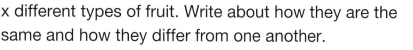 **Write About Differences** Cut out or draw pictures of six different types of fruit. Write about how they are the same and how they differ from one another.

**267**

# The Church in Bolivia

**Focus** How does the Church include different cultures?

In the following story told by a Maryknoll missionary, you will find some ways that the Church in Bolivia is like your parish and some ways that it is different from your parish.

### A REAL-LIFE STORY

## A Floating Church

Our Parish boat

I work with other missionaries in the jungle region of northeast Bolivia. We travel in our parish boat to visit the people who live far apart along the Beni River. Most of the people work deep in the jungle. Some work with rubber trees, and others harvest Brazilian nuts. On our way up the river, we tell whoever is home to gather their neighbors together for Mass, Baptisms, and marriages on the day we will return downstream. When we return, the people gather near the river. There we baptize people, celebrate Mass, and perform marriages.

## The People

The people are happy to have us come and celebrate the sacraments with them. Ninety-five percent of Bolivians are Catholic. Their ancestors were converted to Christianity a long time ago. Many of the people we meet along the river still speak their native Indian languages. The people we meet also bring some of their native customs into their religious life.

❓ **What about the missionaries' experience in Bolivia is different from the experience in your parish?**

## The Mission

My coworkers and I have learned the languages of the people. We spend time talking and listening to the people. We are able to help them take care of their health in a clinic, and we educate them in a school. We have helped them set up a type of company called a *cooperative,* which is owned by the people who use its services. For example, we helped the farmers set up a cooperative so that they could get fair prices for their rubber and nut crops.

Bolivia has a lot of troubles. Once there was an uprising in a town, and one of the government people asked me to be mayor for four months. Another time I was arrested with another priest. We were put in jail because we had helped the people form a cooperative.

Our outdoor clinic

The Beni River

### Activity Share Your Faith

**Reflect:** Think about how the "floating church" is the same as your parish church.

**Share:** With a partner, use examples from the story to describe how the Church includes different cultures.

**Act:** Write one thing that you can do to support people in the Church who come from different cultures.

_____

_____

# To the Whole World

**Focus** How does the Church reach out to the world?

Catholic missionaries bring the Catholic faith to people all over the world. They are careful to respect and include the customs of different groups in prayer and worship.

The missionaries in Bolivia are preaching the gospel of Jesus in word and deed. Before Jesus ascended into heaven, he gave his Apostles this command.

## Faith Fact

There are over 92,000 Catholic missionaries working around the world.

## ✝ SCRIPTURE                                    Matthew 28:18–20

### Go Forth

"All power in heaven and on earth has been given to me. Go, therefore, and make disciples of all nations, baptizing them in the name of the Father, and of the Son, and of the holy Spirit, teaching them to observe all that I have commanded you. And behold, I am with you always, until the end of the age."

*Matthew 28:18–20*

Jesus wanted his followers to go out to all places. Today, no matter where you go in the world, you will find followers of Jesus. In every country, you will find communities of Catholics and other Christians. Every one of these communities and all of the followers of Jesus are called to continue the **mission** of Jesus.

❓ **How do you live out the mission of Jesus?**

## Jesus' Universal Mission

Jesus' universal, or worldwide, mission on earth was to share God's love with all people. When you read the Scriptures, you see that Jesus reached out to all people, especially people who were poor and those who were left out by others. Jesus healed, forgave, and loved people, especially those people who were considered sinners. Jesus treated everyone with dignity and respect. Jesus' mission was one of **justice**.

## Diversity in the Church

There are differences in the way the people of other countries and cultures practice their faith. Even in your parish you may notice a **diversity**, or variety, in the ways that people express their faith. These differences do not divide the Church. They make it better. The Church is united because of its faithfulness to the common belief handed down from the Apostles through their successors, the bishops. The Church is united in the celebration of the Mass, in the Sacraments, in prayer, and when people in every culture help bring justice to the world. You bring justice to the world by working to give others what is rightfully theirs.

❓ **What cultural practices does your parish or family have?**

**Activity** — Connect Your Faith

**Tell the World** Write a newspaper headline that tells one way that you can bring justice to the world now or in the future.

_____

_____

# Helping the Missions

 **Focus** How can you help missionaries spread God's word?

Jesus told his Apostles to go and spread his message all around the world. Today, missionaries continue this work in all corners of the world.

Missionaries give up their lives of comfort to live with and help people in need. The missions provide food, medical care, and education in addition to spreading the word of God. Many missions have very little money to buy the items needed to care for the people. Below are some ways you can help missionaries in their good work.

## Ways to Help

**RAISE MONEY**
Organize projects to raise money to help missionaries purchase supplies.

**COLLECT MEDICAL SUPPLIES**
Collect bandages, first aid cream, old eyeglasses, or cough syrup.

**SEND YOUR SUPPORT**
Write a letter to a missionary, thanking him or her for doing God's work.

**GATHER BIBLES**
Collect Bibles or old hymnbooks to help missions share the word of the Lord.

**PRAY FOR A MISSIONARY**
Say a prayer to bless a missionary and the work that he or she is doing.

❓ **If you were a missionary, what work would you like to do, and where?**

# Live Your Faith

**Design a Care Package**  Missionaries are often gone from home for a long time. What might they need or want? Make a list of the items that you would include in a care package to a missionary. The package may have to travel very far, so don't include anything that can spoil.

# Prayer of Praise

 **Let Us Pray**

*Gather and begin with the Sign of the Cross.*

 *Sing together.*

Go out to all the world, and tell the Good News.

"Psalm 117: Go Out to All the World" © 1969, 1981, and 1997, ICEL.

**Leader:** Lord, all the nations praise you. All the people of the world glorify you.

**All:** God our loving Father, we thank you for the gift of your Son, Jesus. We thank you for the beautiful diversity of our world. All nations and people show us your greatness. Fill us with your Spirit so that we can bring the Good News of Jesus to all whom we meet. Amen.

**A** **Work with Words**   Complete each sentence with the correct word from the Word Bank.

WORD BANK

justice
world
mission
diversity
respect

1. Jesus' _____ was to share God's love with all people.

2. The Church is one, made up of a great _____ of members.

3. The mission of every person in the Church is to bring the good news of Jesus to the _____.

4. The virtue of _____ challenges followers of Jesus to work to provide for the needs and rights of others.

5. Missionaries must _____ the culture and customs of the local people.

**B** **Check Understanding**   List five things that missionaries do for the people they serve.

6. _____

7. _____

8. _____

9. _____

10. _____

## Catholics Believe

- The mission of the People of God is to proclaim the Gospel and to work for the good of all people.

- The Church is made up of people of many cultures, but all are united by their belief in Christ.

### SCRIPTURE

Read *Ephesians 4:7–16* to find out about unity in diversity.

**GO online** www.osvcurriculum.com
For weekly scripture readings and seasonal resources

## Activity

# Live Your Faith

**Research Religious Traditions** Share your experiences of different religious traditions. If possible, go online with a family member to research the religious traditions from a culture other than your own. Plan a special family time to tell what you discovered.

# People of Faith

As a child, **Cesar Chavez** was a migrant farm worker. As an adult, he improved working conditions for migrant workers and started the United Farm Workers union. Cesar had a deep Christian faith. He also followed the nonviolent teachings of Mohandas Gandhi and of Martin Luther King, Jr. He and other protesters often went to Mass together before they began a march. He organized strikes and boycotts to get fair wages for farm workers.

▲ Cesar Chavez
1927–1993

## Family Prayer

Dear God, give us a sense of justice and the courage to carry out your mission of justice in our world as Cesar Chavez did. Amen.

*In Unit 7 your child is learning about the KINGDOM OF GOD.*

# Chapter 21 I Want to See God

## Let Us Pray

**Leader:** God, teach us to live so that we may share eternal life with you.

"Turn from evil and do good;
seek peace and pursue it."

*Psalm 34:15*

**All:** God, teach us to live so that we may share eternal life with you. Amen.

### Activity

## Let's Begin

● **With Jesus** Jessie sat with her mother in the car. Her mother wiped away Jessie's tears and said, "I will miss your Grandma Ruth, too. But she is happy and in heaven with Jesus."

When they arrived at the funeral home, Jessie gazed around the room where the body of her grandmother lay. Sweet-smelling flowers filled the room, and soft music played. With a huge gasp, Jessie declared, "Oh, so this is heaven!"

Now think about heaven.

• Whom would you like to meet in heaven?

_____

_____

✏ **Write About Heaven** Write and illustrate a poem about heaven.

# Being with God

 **Focus** How do the gifts of the Holy Spirit help you live in friendship with God?

Heaven is not a room with sweet-smelling flowers. It is not a place in the sky among the clouds. **Heaven** is the life that all holy people will share with God forever.

To spend eternity with God, you first must grow in friendship with God. Through the Holy Spirit, God has given you gifts that will help you grow in friendship with him and with others. You receive the gifts of the Holy Spirit at Baptism, and in Confirmation these gifts are strengthened in you. These seven powerful gifts help you follow Jesus more closely. They open your heart so that the Holy Spirit can guide you to make good and unselfish choices.

| THE GIFT OF | HELPS YOU |
|---|---|
| WISDOM | • see yourself as God sees you and act as God wants you to act<br>• live in the image and likeness of God |
| UNDERSTANDING | • get to know God, yourself, and other people better<br>• see why you sometimes make wrong choices<br>• learn to make better choices<br>• learn to forgive more freely |
| COUNSEL (or right judgment) | • give good advice to others<br>• hear the Holy Spirit, who speaks to you through your conscience and through the good advice and good example of others |

| THE GIFT OF | HELPS YOU |
|---|---|
| **FORTITUDE** (or courage) | • stand up for what is right even when doing so is difficult<br>• face and overcome your fear, which is sometimes the reason why you make a bad choice or fail to act in loving ways |
| **KNOWLEDGE** | • be open to God's loving communication, or revelation<br>• know God in the way that you come to know someone you love and someone who loves you |
| **PIETY** (or reverence) | • show faithful love and honor to God<br>• recognize the importance of spending time talking and listening to God in prayer<br>• show respect to others because all people are children of God |
| **FEAR OF THE LORD** (or wonder and awe) | • know that God is greater and more wonderful than any created thing<br>• remember to be open to the surprising and powerful goodness of God |

## Activity — Share Your Faith

**Reflect:** Think about times when you used the gifts of the Holy Spirit.

**Share:** With a partner, discuss one of those times.

**Act:** Write one of these gifts in the box on the left, and describe how you use this gift in your everyday life.

# The Last Judgment

**Focus** How does a person prepare for the last judgment?

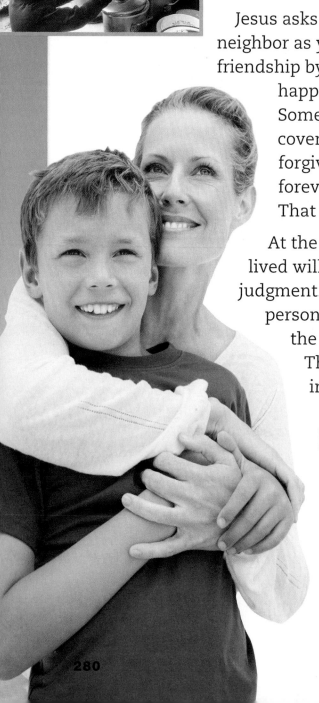

The gifts of the Holy Spirit help you turn away from selfish actions and prepare you to be with God forever. All through your life you have the choice of accepting or rejecting the grace offered through Jesus. At the time of your death, God will judge how well you have accepted his gifts. This is called the **particular judgment**.

Jesus asks you to love God above all things and your neighbor as yourself. If you remain in God's grace and friendship by following his law, the everlasting happiness of heaven will eventually be yours. Some people sin greatly and reject God's covenant of love. They refuse his grace and forgiveness. These sinners will be separated forever from God because of their own choices. That separation is called hell.

At the end of time, all people who have ever lived will rise again and appear before God for judgment. This **last judgment** will not change each person's particular judgment. Rather, it will mark the coming of God's kingdom in its fullness. This is the time when Christ will come again in glory.

## Preparing for Heaven

When you live with the particular and last judgments in mind, you will try to work every day for the justice, love, and peace of God's reign. As you do so, you are preparing to live forever with God. Jesus told his followers what would happen on the day of the last judgment.

# The Last Judgment

"Then the king will say to those on his right, '. . . . Inherit the kingdom prepared for you. . . . For I was hungry and you gave me food, I was thirsty and you gave me drink, a stranger and you welcomed me, naked and you clothed me, ill and you cared for me, in prison and you visited me.' Then the righteous will answer him and say, 'Lord, when did we see you hungry and feed you, or thirsty and give you drink? When did we see you a stranger and welcome you, or naked and clothe you? When did we see you ill or in prison, and visit you?' And the king will say to them in reply, 'Amen, I say to you, whatever you did for one of these least brothers of mine, you did for me.' "

*Matthew 25:34–40*

## Words of Faith

**Particular judgment** is the individual judgment by God at the time of your death.

The **last judgment** will occur at the end of time when Jesus returns to judge all who have ever lived. Then, all will fully see and understand God's plan for creation.

❓ **Who is the king in this story?**

❓ **Who are the righteous in this story?**

## Activity    Connect Your Faith

**Express Yourself**  Make a slogan for a bumper sticker about living according to how you will be judged. Then decorate the bumper sticker with markers or colored pencils.

281

# Prepare to Meet God

 **Focus** How can you grow in friendship with God?

God our Father, by the Holy Spirit, has given you seven powerful gifts to help you grow in friendship with him. He is always there to help and encourage you as you learn to use these gifts in your life. Using them will help you be ready when you finally meet God.

## Grow in God's Love

Sometimes you might feel lonely or unsure of what you should do. During these times, you can reach out to God and to others. Here are some examples.

**Look for Guidance**
When you are faced with a difficult choice, remember the gifts of the Holy Spirit. Pray for the Spirit's help.

**Give Thanks**
When you feel joy or happiness, thank God, the source of all goodness.

**Reach Out**
When you meet a person who is lonely, afraid, or suffering, reach out with words and actions of love.

**Stop and Pray**
When you are rushed or stressed, stop and pray. Feel God's presence and find comfort.

**Notice the Beauty**
When you experience sadness, look around at the beauty of God's creation and the blessings you have been given.

❓ **What are other times to reach out to God?**

# Live Your Faith

**Plan a Skit**  Write a skit about meeting God. Where will you meet him? Will anyone else be there? What will you say?

Title: _____

Setting: _____

_____

Characters: _____

_____

_____

_____

_____

**What God says:** _____

_____

_____

_____

_____

_____

_____

What characters say: _____

_____

_____

_____

_____

_____

_____

_____

_____

# Prayer for the Kingdom

 Let Us Pray

*Gather and begin with the Sign of the Cross.*

**Leader:** Lord Jesus, you sometimes described heaven as a feast or a banquet. Help us remember the gift of your life and teaching that we have shared together this year. Be with us as we remember and pray.

*Share a story of Jesus that you remember from this year. Then pray together.*

**All:** **Lord Jesus, we long to see your face. May your kingdom come into our hearts and into our world. Open our hearts to those who are poor, sick, imprisoned, lonely, and suffering. Make us one Body in Christ through the gifts of your Spirit. Help us ready ourselves for the banquet of heaven. Amen.**

 *Sing together.*

We come to share our story,
*Venimos a decir del misterio,*
we come to break the bread.
*y partir el pan de vida.*
We come to know our rising from the dead.
*Venimos a saber de nuestra eternidad.*

**A** **Work with Words**   Circle the choice that best completes each sentence.

1. (Last/Particular) judgment is the individual judgment by God at the time of your death.

2. The (last/particular) judgment will occur at the end of time when Jesus returns to judge all who have ever lived.

3. A separation from God forever is called (sin/hell).

4. The last judgment (will/will not) change your particular judgment.

5. Heaven is the (state/place) of eternal happiness with God.

**B** **Check Understanding**   For each statement, write the correct gift of the Spirit.

6. Josh gives his best friend good advice, telling him not to shoplift. _____

7. Kim didn't do her homework, but she decides to tell her teacher the truth. _____

8. Tasha was ready to steal a CD. When she remembered what was talked about in religion class, she put the CD back. _____

9. Madison is overwhelmed with the beauty of the night sky, and she thinks of God.

_____

10. Amelia is struggling with a decision. She thinks about what Jesus would do.

_____

UNIT 7: CHAPTER 21

# Family Faith

## Catholics Believe

- The Church teaches that at the end of time, all will be raised from the dead.

- After being raised from the dead, all will come into the presence of Christ to be judged.

### ✝ SCRIPTURE

Read *Mark 7:31–37* to learn a story about Jesus' powerful ability to heal those who are suffering.

**GO online** **www.osvcurriculum.com**
For weekly scripture readings and seasonal resources

## Activity

# Live Your Faith

**Think of Ways to Help** As a family, brainstorm ways in which people in the world are suffering. Look for newspaper articles and stories on the news. When you gather for dinner, pray for a person or about a situation in which there is suffering. Discuss how your family could help. If there is no direct action you can take, keep that person or situation in your family's prayers each day this week.

Daily News

# People of Faith

On May 6, 1984, the Church canonized 103 Korean people. These saints ranged in age from thirteen-year-old **Peter Yu Tae-chol** to seventy-two-year-old **Mark Chong**. Each of these people sacrificed his or her life for the sake of Jesus and the Catholic faith. Eleven of the martyrs were priests. Many of these saints were the first Christians in Korea, among them **Yi Sung-hun**, founder of the first Church community in that country. The feast day for these saints and martyrs is September 20.

▲ Korean Saints and Martyrs 1839–1867

## Family Prayer

Saints and martyrs of Korea, pray for us that we will be strong in our faith even when it is difficult to do so. Pray that we may live wisely and lovingly to prepare to meet God at the end of time. Amen.

*In Unit 7 your child is learning about the KINGDOM OF GOD.*

**286** **CCC** *See Catechism of the Catholic Church 681–682 for further reading on chapter content.*

# Faith in Action!
## CATHOLIC SOCIAL TEACHING

In this unit, you learned that God created the goods of the earth to benefit the whole human family. During his time on earth, Jesus was a friend to the people who had little money or power. One way to live out the mission of Jesus is by helping those who are poor.

## Option for the Poor

The crowds that came to hear Jesus preach included many people who were poor or sick. Jesus wanted his Church to be a Church for the poor. Jesus told people who were poor that they were blessed in God's eyes. God's kingdom belonged to them.

For Catholics, the needs of those who are poor come first. Every Catholic parish is called to serve people who are poor. This is a job that parishioners must do in order to live their faith.

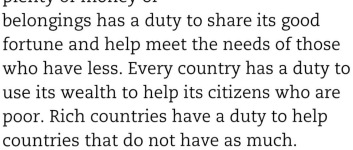

A family that has plenty of money or belongings has a duty to share its good fortune and help meet the needs of those who have less. Every country has a duty to use its wealth to help its citizens who are poor. Rich countries have a duty to help countries that do not have as much.

❓ **What are some ways that families, parishes, and countries could show that they put the needs of the poor first?**

# The People Outside

Jesus reached out to the poor and asks you to do the same. Let's see how one parish is following Jesus' example.

One fall, as it was turning cold, members of Old St. Joseph's Church in Pennsylvania noticed that homeless people were sleeping on sidewalks near the church. Parish volunteers organized a "Carewalk." Twice a week, parishioners walked around the neighborhood, giving hot soup, warm clothes, and blankets to the homeless people. When more parishioners volunteered, the parish stopped the Carewalks to serve hot lunches in the church basement every weekday.

## Continuing to Care

Some time later, the church building had to be closed for many months because its old roof leaked. During the repairs, no meals could be cooked or served in the church. Many homeless people depended on the hot meals. The parish couldn't just forget about these people until the repairs were finished.

After praying and talking, the people of the parish remembered the Carewalks. They decided to start them again. On four evenings of each week, parishioners took bag dinners to people in the neighborhood who were homeless, to make up for the missed lunches.

❷ Why did the parishioners of Old St. Joseph's feel it was important continue with Carewalks?

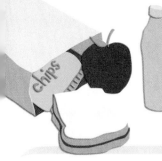

# Reach out!

## How Can You Help?

The parishioners of Old St. Joseph have chosen to follow Jesus' example of putting other peoples' needs before their own.

Tell about a time when you put the needs of others before your own.

_____

_____

_____

What good thing happened because of your action?

_____

_____

_____

Think of ways that you or a group to which you belong might help in the following situations.

A friend lost her lunch money.

_____

_____

A woman is poor and has a sick child.

_____

_____

A homeless person is outside on a cold night.

_____

_____

## Make a Difference

**Write About Needs** What would life be like if you were homeless? Write a story titled "My Day as a Homeless Person." Imagine that you have been living on the streets for a week. Write about what you would do for one full day. Include how you obtain food, shelter, and medical care and what happens during the day. Read your story to the class. Then together pray a prayer telling God how you will remember the needs of those who are poor.

**A** **Work with Words**   Complete each sentence with the correct term.

1. To _____ or want for yourself what belongs to others is called envy.

2. Variety, especially among people, is known as

   _____.

3. The _____ will occur at the end of time, when Jesus returns to judge all who have ever lived.

4. The virtue of giving to God and people what is due them is called

   _____.

5. _____ is the desire to acquire earthly goods without limit or beyond one's means.

6. The _____ are those who do not become too attached to their possessions and are able to help bring about God's reign.

7. To share the good news of Jesus and the kingdom of God, people

   are sent on a _____.

8. _____ is the responsibility to care for all of God's creation.

9. The state of eternal happiness with God is known as

   _____.

10. _____ is the individual judgment by God at the time of a person's death.

## B Check Understanding    Fill in the circle next to the answer that best completes each statement.

**11.** In the story of King Midas, the king learned not to put his desire for

_____ first.

○ food            ○ his daughter        ○ riches

**12.** _____ left their homes, families, and jobs in order to follow Jesus and help him spread God's word.

○ The Israelites      ○ Adam and Eve        ○ The Apostles

**13.** Missionaries follow Jesus' example by reaching out to

_____ people, especially those who are sick and those who are poor.

○ most            ○ all              ○ some

**14.** Being separated from God forever as a result of a person's choice to sin and reject his forgiveness is called _____.

○ hell            ○ greed            ○ heaven

**15.** You received the seven gifts of the Holy Spirit at Baptism, including

_____.

○ wisdom          ○ piety            ○ both are correct

## C Make Connections    Use the five words listed below to write a brief paragraph that answers the following question: What can you do in your life now to prepare for when you will see God?

generous     mission     heaven     judgment     Holy Spirit

**16.–20.** _____

_____

_____

_____

_____

_____

# CATHOLIC SOURCE BOOK

## The Books of the Bible

The Catholic version of the Bible contains seventy-three books—forty-six in the Old Testament and twenty-seven in the New Testament.

### The Old Testament

#### The Pentateuch

| | | |
|---|---|---|
| Genesis | Leviticus | Deuteronomy |
| Exodus | Numbers | |

#### The Historical Books

| | | |
|---|---|---|
| Joshua | 2 Kings | Judith |
| Judges | 1 Chronicles | Esther |
| Ruth | 2 Chronicles | 1 Maccabees |
| 1 Samuel | Ezra | 2 Maccabees |
| 2 Samuel | Nehemiah | |
| 1 Kings | Tobit | |

#### The Wisdom Books

| | | |
|---|---|---|
| Job | Ecclesiastes | Sirach |
| Psalms | Song of Songs | (Ecclesiasticus) |
| Proverbs | Wisdom | |

## Faith Fact

Before the invention of the printing press, the Bible had to be copied by hand. Many times when copying the text, monks would also illuminate, or illustrate, Scripture passages.

## The Prophetic Books

| | | |
|---|---|---|
| Isaiah | Hosea | Nahum |
| Jeremiah | Joel | Habakkuk |
| Lamentations | Amos | Zephaniah |
| Baruch | Obadiah | Haggai |
| Ezekiel | Jonah | Zechariah |
| Daniel | Micah | Malachi |

# The New Testament

## The Gospels

Matthew
Mark
Luke
John

## The New Testament Letters

| | | |
|---|---|---|
| Romans | 1 Thessalonians | James |
| 1 Corinthians | 2 Thessalonians | 1 Peter |
| 2 Corinthians | 1 Timothy | 2 Peter |
| Galatians | 2 Timothy | 1 John |
| Ephesians | Titus | 2 John |
| Philippians | Philemon | 3 John |
| Colossians | Hebrews | Jude |

## The Acts of the Apostles

## Revelation

## Scripture

### Faith Fact

Each of the Gospel writers has a symbol. Matthew is represented by a winged man, Mark is represented by a winged lion, Luke is represented by a winged ox, and John is represented by an eagle.

## About the Old Testament

**The Pentateuch** is the first five books of the Old Testament. The word pentateuch means "five containers." In the beginning the pentateuch was written on leather or papyrus and each book was kept in a separate container. Jewish people call these books the Torah. The books of the pentateuch tell of the beginning of human relationship with God. They also tell the story of God's loving actions for humans.

The Wisdom books of the Old Testament provide guidance in human behavior. Wisdom is a spiritual gift that allows a person to know God's purpose and plan. They remind us that God's wisdom is always greater than human knowledge.

Many prophets were authors of Old Testament books. A prophet is a person sent by God to call people back to their covenant with God.

## The Formation of the New Testament

The New Testament was formed in three stages:

1. The life and teaching of Jesus—Jesus' whole life and teaching proclaimed the good news.
2. The oral tradition—After the Resurrection the Apostles preached the good news. Then the early Christians passed on what the Apostles had preached. They told and retold the teachings of Jesus and the story of his life, death, and Resurrection.
3. The four Gospels and other writings—The stories, teachings, and sayings of Jesus were collected and written down in the Gospels according to Matthew, Mark, Luke, and John. The actions and lessons of the early Church were recorded in the Acts of the Apostles and the New Testament letters.

# How to Locate Bible Passages

To practice finding a particular Bible passage, use the example of *Matthew 8:23–27*.

*Matthew* is the name of a book in the Bible. The chapter number always comes directly after the name of the book, so 8 is the chapter number. The numbers 23–27 refer to the verses. To find this passage, go to the table of contents in your Bible. Find the page number for the Gospel according to Matthew, and turn to that page. The chapter number will be at the top of the page. Turn the pages to find Chapter 8. When you reach Chapter 8, look for the smaller numbers within the passage. These are the verse numbers. Find verse 23. This is where you will begin reading. Continue reading through verse 27, the last verse in the passage.

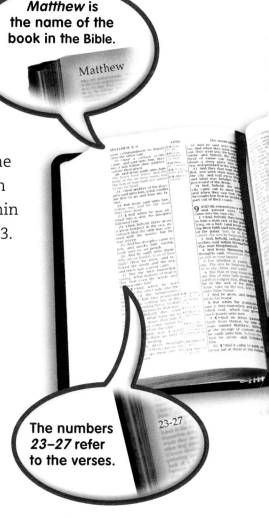

*Matthew* is the name of the book in the Bible.

The numbers *23–27* refer to the verses.

# The Covenant

**The covenant** is the sacred agreement joining God and humans in relationship. When God made the covenant with Noah after the flood, he promised never to destroy the earth again. God renewed the covenant with Abram (Abraham), promising that Abraham's descendants would be as numerous as the stars. Years later, when the descendants of Abraham were slaves in Egypt, God used Moses to lead the people away in the *Exodus*, or "the road out." At Mount Sinai the covenant was renewed with Moses. God guided the Israelites to the Promised Land. In return, the Israelites were called to love only God and to follow his Law, the Ten Commandments. Finally, through the Paschal mystery—Jesus' life, death, and Resurrection—the covenant was fulfilled and a new covenant was created. The new covenant is open to all who remain faithful to God.

# The Holy Trinity

God is revealed in three Persons: God the Father and Creator, God the Son and Savior, God the Holy Spirit and Guide. Each of the Persons of the Trinity is separate from the other Persons. However, the Father, Son, and Holy Spirit are one and the same God. The Holy Trinity is the central mystery of the Catholic faith.

The mission of God the Son and God the Holy Spirit is to bring people into the love of the Trinity—the perfect love that exists in the Father, Son, and Holy Spirit.

## God the Father

God created all things. The beauty of creation reflects the beauty of the Creator. He cares for and loves all. In his divine providence, God guides everything toward himself.

## God the Son

Jesus is the Son of God. The Church has many important teachings about him. The **Incarnation** is a basic mystery of the Catholic faith and is the belief that God became man. Jesus Christ became man in order to save all people from the power of sin and everlasting death. Jesus was truly man and yet was truly God. Jesus became human, being born of the Virgin Mary. Except for sin, Jesus had all the experiences of being human.

Through the teachings of Jesus, people come to know about the kingdom of God and how to live for God's reign. From the Sermon on the Mount and other teachings, people learn to live in love. Jesus did not reject sinners, but instead called them to turn away from sin and back to God. Jesus taught everyone how to live the Ten Commandments—by loving God and all of his creation.

## Faith Fact

The Holy Trinity is represented by many symbols, including the equilateral triangle, three interwoven circles, a circle of three fish, and the shamrock.

Jesus' **Resurrection** showed him as the Messiah, the Savior. By his death Jesus conquered sin. By rising from the dead, Jesus conquered death and so saved all humans from the power of sin and everlasting death.

The Ascension happened forty days after the Resurrection, when Jesus ascended to heaven to join the glory of God the Father. At the Ascension Jesus commanded the Apostles to continue his mission by teaching and guiding people toward God's kingdom. The sending of the Holy Spirit on Pentecost is the final part of Jesus' act of salvation.

## God the Holy Spirit

The Holy Spirit continues to guide people in the Christian life. Through the teachings of Jesus, Christians learned how to live in love. Through the strength and wisdom of the Holy Spirit, they are able to lead this life of love. The Holy Spirit breathes into the faithful his fruits and his gifts. The fruits—such as piety, peace, and joy—and the gifts—such as wisdom, courage, and reverence—help humans turn toward God and cooperate in bringing about the kingdom of God.

The **Immaculate Conception** means that Mary was preserved from original sin from the first moment of conception. The Feast of the Immaculate Conception is December 8. On this date, the Catholics of Paraguay celebrate the feast day of the Virgin of Caacupe. Centuries ago, the Virgin Mary appeared in the Paraguayan countryside. A church was built in the place where she had appeared, and many pilgrims to that church have experienced miracles. Today December 8 is as special a celebration to the Catholics of Paraguay as Christmas is. Many Paraguayans honor Mary every year by making a pilgrimage, or long walk, to the church of the Virgin of Caacupe.

## Faith Fact

The many titles for the Pope include: Bishop of Rome, Vicar of Christ, Supreme Pontiff of the Universal Church, Patriarch of the West, Primate of Italy, Successor of St. Peter, Prince of the Apostles, Servant of the Servants of God, and Sovereign of Vatican City.

# Church

Church **authority** is based on the command from Jesus to his Apostles to make disciples of people everywhere, teaching them to live as Jesus taught and baptizing them in the name of the Father, Son, and Holy Spirit. (See *Matthew 28:18–20*.) Authority also comes from the Holy Spirit as the Spirit of Truth that guides the Church. The official teaching authority of the Church is the **magisterium,** which is made up of the pope and the bishops. The magisterium teaches with the authority given by Jesus and the guidance of the Holy Spirit.

## Mission

The Church has the mission to help bring justice to everyone. The principles of social justice are respect for all persons, equality for all persons, and oneness in the family of God with responsibility for one another. These principles can be accomplished with the fair distribution of goods, fair wages for work, and fair resolution in conflicts.

## Pope

The pope's title of "Servant of the Servants" began with Pope Gregory the Great. It is stated at Mark 10:44 *"[W]hoever wishes to be first among you will be the slave of all."*

## Saints

Canonization is the process by which the Church recognizes faithful people as saints. During each of the three stages of becoming a saint, the faithful person has a different title—first Venerable, then Blessed, and finally Saint.

# Last Things

## Purgatory

At death some people are not ready for heaven and God's eternal friendship. However, they have not broken their relationship with God. These souls are given time in purgatory. *Purgatory* means "purifying." Purgatory helps the soul prepare for life with God. The soul becomes more faithful and loving.

## Particular judgment

When people die, they are judged by how well they have lived and loved. This judgment is called particular judgment. Souls will be given reward or punishment at this time.

## General judgment

General judgment, or the last judgment, will occur at the Second Coming of Christ. This judgment represents God's triumph over evil. General judgment will mark the arrival of God's kingdom in its fullness. General judgment will happen to all people, living and dead. However, this judgment will not change the particular judgment received by each soul.

# The Liturgical Year

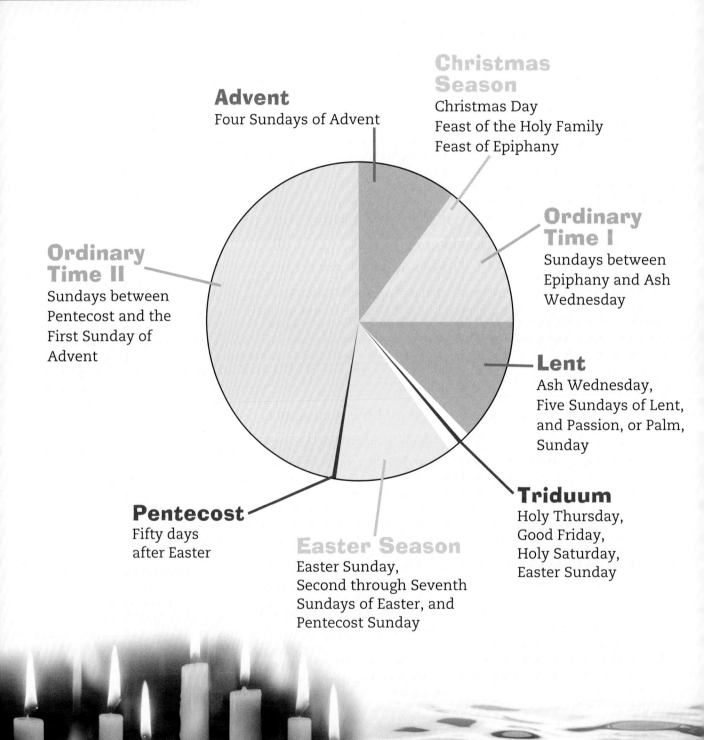

**Advent**
Four Sundays of Advent

**Christmas Season**
Christmas Day
Feast of the Holy Family
Feast of Epiphany

**Ordinary Time I**
Sundays between Epiphany and Ash Wednesday

**Ordinary Time II**
Sundays between Pentecost and the First Sunday of Advent

**Lent**
Ash Wednesday, Five Sundays of Lent, and Passion, or Palm, Sunday

**Triduum**
Holy Thursday, Good Friday, Holy Saturday, Easter Sunday

**Pentecost**
Fifty days after Easter

**Easter Season**
Easter Sunday, Second through Seventh Sundays of Easter, and Pentecost Sunday

## Lent

Lent is a time of fasting, prayer, and almsgiving. The forty days of Lent remind Christians of the number of days Jesus spent fasting in the desert. The forty days also represent the number of years the Israelites spent wandering in the desert after the Exodus.

Lent begins with Ash Wednesday, a day of penance. The last Friday in Lent, Good Friday, is also a day of penance. All Catholics from their eighteenth to their fifty-ninth birthdays must fast on days of penance: They eat light meals and have no food between meals. On Ash Wednesday and on all Fridays during Lent, abstinence is required for Catholics fourteen years of age or older. This means that they may not eat meat. Fasting, abstinence, and personal reflection during Lent help prepare Catholics for the celebration of Easter.

## The Triduum

The *Triduum*, which means "three days," starts with the celebration of the Lord's Supper on Holy Thursday. Good Friday is observed with a Liturgy of the Word, Veneration of the Cross, and a Communion service. On Holy Saturday evening the Easter Vigil is celebrated. The Triduum ends with evening prayer on Easter Sunday. Because the Triduum celebrates the Paschal mystery—the life, death, and Resurrection of Jesus—it is the high point of the entire Church year.

## Faith Fact

The palms from Palm Sunday are collected and burned. The ashes are then used for the following year's Ash Wednesday service.

# The Sacraments

The Catholic Church celebrates seven Sacraments, or signs, of Jesus' presence. There are three groups of Sacraments.

| | |
|---|---|
| **Sacraments of Initiation** | Baptism Confirmation Eucharist |
| **Sacraments of Healing** | Reconciliation Anointing of the Sick |
| **Sacraments of Vocation and Service** | Matrimony Holy Orders |

## Holy Water

Holy water is water that has been blessed. It is used during the Sacrament of Baptism as well as for the blessing of people or objects. Fonts of holy water are placed at the entrances of churches so that people may bless themselves and recall the meaning of Baptism as they make the Sign of the Cross.

## The Paschal Candle

The Paschal candle is a symbol of Christ and of Easter. This candle is lit from the Easter fire during the Easter Vigil. Throughout the fifty days of the Easter Season, the candle burns during the liturgy. After the Easter Season it is used during baptisms and funerals as a symbol of the Resurrection.

# The Sacrament of Reconciliation

The Sacrament of Reconciliation is also known as the Sacrament of Penance or the Sacrament of Confession. In this Sacrament, sin is forgiven and the one who has sinned is reconciled with God, with himself or herself, and with the Church community. The essential elements for Reconciliation are

- contrition (sorrow for the sin)
- confession
- absolution by the priest
- satisfaction (attempting to correct or undo the wrong done). The priest can never reveal what he is told during a confession. The priest's silence is called the *sacramental seal* or the *seal of confession.*

## Celebrating the Sacrament

### Communal Rite of Reconciliation

1. Greeting
2. Celebration of the Word
3. Homily
4. Examination of Conscience
5. General Confession of Sin
6. The Lord's Prayer
7. Individual Confession of Sins, Acceptance of a penance, and Absolution
8. Closing Prayer

### Individual Rite of Reconciliation

1. Welcome
2. Reading from Scripture
3. Confession of Sins and Acceptance of a Penance
4. Act of Contrition
5. Absolution
6. Closing Prayer

# Morality

## The Beatitudes

The Beatitudes are sayings of Jesus that show us the way to true happiness in God's kingdom. The Beatitudes are listed in the Gospel according to Matthew (*Matthew* 5:3–10), see Chapter 7.

## The New Commandment

Jesus also gave his followers a new commandment: "love one another. As I have loved you, so you also should love one another." (*John* 13:34).

## Faith Fact

The eight points on the Maltese Cross represent the Beatitudes.

## The Ten Commandments

| THE TEN COMMANDMENTS | THEIR MEANING |
|---|---|
| 1. I am the Lord your God. You shall not have strange Gods before me. | Keep God first in your life. |
| 2. You shall not take the name of the Lord your God in vain. | Always use God's name in a reverent way. |
| 3. Remember to keep holy the Lord's day. | Attend Mass and rest on Sunday. |
| 4. Honor your mother and father. | Obey your father and mother. |
| 5. You shall not kill. | Care for yourself and others. |
| 6. You shall not commit adultery. | Be respectful of every person. |
| 7. You shall not steal. | Respect other people and their property. |
| 8. You shall not bear false witness against your neighbor. | Respect others by always telling the truth. |
| 9. You shall not covet your neighbor's wife. | Don't be jealous of other people's relationships. |
| 10. You shall not covet your neighbor's goods. | Don't be jealous of what other people have. |

# Conscience

Conscience is the gift from God that helps you know the difference between right and wrong. Conscience helps you choose what is right. It involves free will and reason working together. You must form your conscience properly. If not formed properly, your conscience can lead you to choose what is wrong.

Forming your conscience is a lifelong process. It involves practicing virtues and avoiding sin and people or situations that may lead you to sin. You can turn to good people for advice, to Church teachings for guidance, and to God for help in educating your conscience.

## Examining Your Conscience

For help with examining your conscience, use the following steps:

1. Pray for the Holy Spirit's help in making a fresh start.

2. Look at your life in the light of the Beatitudes, the Ten Commandments, the Great Commandment, and the precepts of the Church.

3. Ask yourself these questions:
   Where have I fallen short of what God wants for me? Whom have I hurt? What have I done that I knew was wrong? What have I not done that I should have done? Have I made the necessary changes in bad habits? What areas am I still having trouble with? Am I sincerely sorry for all my sins?

# Law

Laws are rules that help people live as members of a community and behave in an acceptable manner.

**Divine law** is the eternal law of God. It includes physical law and moral law. The law of gravity is an example of physical. A moral law is one that humans understand through reasoning (you may not steal) and through divine revelation (keep holy the Lord's Day).

**Natural moral law** consists of those decisions and duties that all humans accept as right. For example, people everywhere understand that no one may kill another unjustly. Everyone must obey natural moral law.

## Precepts of the Church

The following precepts are important duties of all Catholics.

1. Take part in the Mass on Sundays and holy days. Keep these days holy and avoid unnecessary work.
2. Celebrate the Sacrament of Reconciliation at least once a year.
3. Receive Holy Communion at least once a year during Easter Season.
4. Fast and abstain on days of penance.
5. Give your time, gifts, and money to support the Church.

## Corporal Works of Mercy

These works of mercy help care for the physical needs of others.

Feed the hungry.
Give drink to the thirsty.
Clothe the naked.
Shelter the homeless.
Visit the sick.
Visit the imprisoned.
Bury the dead.

## Human Dignity

God's image is his likeness that is present in you because you are his creation. You are called to respect the dignity of all people because everyone is made in God's image.

## Freedom

Freedom means you are able to choose and act with few limitations.

## Free will

Free will is the gift from God that allows humans to make their own choices. Because you are free to choose between right and wrong, you are responsible for your choices and actions.

## Grace

God gives you two types of grace. **Sanctifying grace** is the gift of God's life in you. It gives you the desire to live and act within God's plan. **Actual grace** is the gift of God's life in you that helps you think or act in a particular situation according to God's plan. Actual grace opens you to understanding and strengthens your will.

## Gifts of the Holy Spirit

You receive the gifts of the Holy Spirit through the Sacraments of Baptism and Confirmation. These gifts help you grow in relationship with God and others.

| | |
|---|---|
| Wisdom | Knowledge |
| Understanding | Reverence *(Piety)* |
| Right judgment *(Counsel)* | Wonder and awe *(Fear of* |
| Courage *(Fortitude)* | *the Lord)* |

# Sin

Sin is a turning away from God and a failure to love others. Sin affects both the individual and the community. A person may be sorry for his or her sin, ask forgiveness for it, accept punishment for it, and resolve to do better. In this case, the experience may actually help the person develop as a Christian and avoid sin in the future. However, a person who makes a habit of sin will harm his or her development, set a poor example, and bring sorrow to others. Society suffers when people disobey God's law and the just laws of society. There are many types of sin.

**Original Sin** is the human condition of weakness and the tendency toward sin that resulted from the first humans' choice to disobey God. Baptism restores the relationship of loving grace in which all people were created.

**Actual sin** is any thought, word, act, or failure to act that goes against God's law. Sin is always a choice, never a mistake.

**Mortal sin** separates you from God. A mortal sin is an act, such as murder. There must be a deliberate choice to commit the act; it is never an accident.

**Venial sin** does not destroy your relationship with God, but it does weaken the relationship. Venial sin often comes from bad habits. It can lead to mortal sin.

**Social sin** happens when one person's sins affect the larger community. Poverty and racism are examples of social sin.

# Virtue

Virtues are good qualities or habits of goodness. These are the two types of virtues:

## Faith Fact

The word *virtue* means "strength." Practicing virtue can give you the strength to make loving choices.

| Theological Virtues | Cardinal Virtues |
| --- | --- |
| Faith | Prudence (careful judgment) |
| Hope | Fortitude (courage) |
| Love | Justice (giving people their due) |
| | Temperance (moderation, balance) |

# The Sign of the Cross

In the name of the Father, and of the Son, and of the Holy Spirit. Amen.

# The Lord's Prayer

Our Father,
   who art in heaven,
hallowed be thy name;
thy kingdom come;
thy will be done on earth
   as it is in heaven.
Give us this day our
   daily bread;
and forgive us our
   trespasses
as we forgive those who trespass
      against us;
and lead us not into temptation,
but deliver us from evil. Amen.

# Hail Mary

Hail, Mary, full of grace,
the Lord is with you!
Blessed are you among women,
and blessed is the fruit of your womb, Jesus.
Holy Mary, Mother of God,
pray for us sinners,
now and at the hour of our death. Amen.

# Glory to the Father (Doxology)

Glory to the Father, and to the Son, and to the Holy Spirit:
as it was in the beginning, is now, and will be forever. Amen.

# Apostles' Creed

I believe in God, the Father almighty,
Creator of heaven and earth,
and in Jesus Christ, his only Son, our Lord,

*At the words that follow, up to and including the Virgin Mary, all bow.*

who was conceived by the Holy Spirit,
born of the Virgin Mary,
suffered under Pontius Pilate,
was crucified, died and was buried;

he descended into hell;
on the third day he rose again from the dead;
he ascended into heaven,
and is seated at the right hand of God the Father almighty;
from there he will come to judge the living and the dead.

I believe in the Holy Spirit,
the holy catholic Church,
the communion of saints,
the forgiveness of sins,
the resurrection of the body,
and life everlasting. Amen.

## Faith Fact

*Amen* means "So be it."
Isn't that the perfect way
to end a conversation
with God?

# Nicene Creed

I believe in one God,
the Father almighty,
maker of heaven and earth,
of all things visible and invisible.
I believe in one Lord Jesus Christ,
the Only Begotten Son of God,
born of the Father before all ages.
God from God, Light from Light,
true God from true God,
begotten, not made,
consubstantial with the Father;
through him all things were made.
For us men and for our salvation
he came down from heaven,

*At the words that follow up to and including and became man, all bow.*

and by the Holy Spirit was incarnate of the Virgin Mary,
and became man.
For our sake he was crucified under Pontius Pilate,
he suffered death and was buried,
and rose again on the third day
in accordance with the Scriptures.
He ascended into heaven
and is seated at the right hand of the Father.
He will come again in glory to judge the living and the dead

and his kingdom will have no end.
I believe in the Holy Spirit, the Lord, the giver of life,
who proceeds from the Father and the Son,
who with the Father and the Son is adored and glorified,
who has spoken through the prophets.
I believe in one, holy, catholic and apostolic Church.
I confess one Baptism for the forgiveness of sins
and I look forward to the resurrection of the dead
and the life of the world to come. Amen.

# I Confess/Confiteor

I confess to almighty God
and to you, my brothers and sisters,
that I have greatly sinned,
in my thoughts and in my words,
in what I have done
and in what I have failed to do,

*Gently strike your chest with a closed fist.*

through my fault, through my fault,
through my most grievous fault;

*Continue:*

therefore I ask blessed Mary ever-Virgin,
all the Angels and Saints,
and you, my brothers and sisters,
to pray for me to the Lord our God.

# Prayer to the Holy Spirit

Come, Holy Spirit, fill the hearts of your faithful.
And kindle in them the fire of your love.
Send forth your Spirit and they will be created.
And you will renew the face of the earth.
Let us pray.
Lord, by the light of the Holy Spirit you have taught the
hearts of your faithful. In the same Spirit help us to relish
what is right and always rejoice in your consolation. We ask
this through Christ our Lord. Amen.

## Memorare

Remember, most loving Virgin Mary, never was it heard that
anyone who turned to you for help was left unaided. Inspired
by this confidence, though burdened by my sins, I run to your
protection for you are my mother. Mother of the Word of God,
do not despise my words of pleading but be merciful and
hear my prayer. Amen.

# Act of Contrition

My God, I am sorry for my sins with all my heart.
In choosing to do wrong
and failing to do good,
I have sinned against you
whom I should love above all things.
I firmly intend, with your help,
to do penance,
to sin no more,
and to avoid whatever leads me to sin.
Our Savior Jesus Christ
suffered and died for us.
In his name, my God, have mercy.

# Grail Prayer

Lord Jesus,
I give you my hands to do your work.
I give you my feet to go your way.
I give you my eyes to see as you do.
I give you my tongue to speak your words.
I give you my mind that you may think in me.

Above all, I give you my heart
that you may love in me your Father
and all mankind.
I give you my whole self that
you may grow in me,
so that it is you, Lord Jesus,
who will live and work and pray in me. Amen.

## Faith Fact

Contrition is the sorrow
that rises up in the soul,
making you repent past sins
and plan not to sin again.
To repent is to turn back
from the sin and ask God's
mercy.

# Prayer for Our Lady of Guadalupe Day

(December 12)

Loving God,
you bless the peoples of the Americas
with the Virgin Mary of Guadalupe
as our patron and mother.
Through her prayers
may we learn to love one another
and to work for justice and peace.
Amen.

| | |
|---|---|
| Lady of Guadalupe, | **pray for us** |
| La morena of Tepeyac, | **comfort us** |
| Mother of the faithful, | **defend us** |
| Refuge of the oppressed, | **strengthen us** |
| Hope of the immigrant, | **cheer us** |
| Light of the traveler, | **guide us** |
| Friend of the stranger, | **welcome us** |
| Shelter of the poor and needy, | **sustain us** |
| Patron of the Americas, | **unite us** |
| Mother of many children, | **watch over us** |
| Star of the morning, | **waken us to the coming** |
| | **of your Son, Jesus Christ,** |
| | **who arose from you the** |
| | **sun of justice and is Lord** |
| | **for ever and ever. Amen.** |

# Litany of St. Joseph

| | |
|---|---|
| Lord, have mercy. | **Lord, have mercy.** |
| Christ, have mercy. | **Christ, have mercy.** |
| Lord, have mercy. | **Lord, have mercy.** |
| Good Saint Joseph, | **pray for us.** |
| Descendant of the House of David | **pray for us.** |
| Husband of Mary, | **pray for us.** |
| Foster father of Jesus, | **pray for us.** |
| Guardian of Christ, | **pray for us.** |
| Support of the holy family, | **pray for us.** |
| Model of workers, | **pray for us.** |
| Example to parents, | **pray for us.** |
| Comfort of the dying, | **pray for us.** |
| Provider of food to the hungry, | **pray for us.** |
| Companion of the poor, | **pray for us.** |
| Protector of the church, | **pray for us.** |

Merciful God,
grant that we may learn from Saint Joseph
to care for the members of our families
and share what we have with the poor.
We ask this through Christ our Lord. Amen.

# The Way of the Cross

The First Station: Jesus is condemned to death.
The Second Station: Jesus bears his cross.
The Third Station: Jesus falls the first time.
The Fourth Station: Jesus meets his mother.
The Fifth Station: Simon of Cyrene helps Jesus carry his cross.
The Sixth Station: Veronica wipes the face of Jesus.
The Seventh Station: Jesus falls a second time.
The Eighth Station: Jesus meets the women of Jerusalem.
The Ninth Station: Jesus falls a third time.
The Tenth Station: Jesus is stripped of his garments.
The Eleventh Station: Jesus is nailed to the cross.
The Twelfth Station: Jesus dies on the cross.
The Thirteenth Station: Jesus is taken down from the cross.
The Fourteenth Station: Jesus is placed in the tomb.

## Faith Fact

In the devotion known as the Way of the Cross, "stations" represent stops along the way of Jesus' journey from Pilate's court all the way to the tomb. Walking in a church from one station to the next and really focusing on each picture or image of the passion of Christ can inspire prayer from the heart.

# The Mysteries of the Rosary

| The Joyful Mysteries | The Luminous Mysteries |
|---|---|
| The Annunciation | The Baptism of Jesus |
| The Visitation | The Wedding at Cana |
| The Nativity | The Proclamation of the Kingdom |
| The Presentation in the Temple | The Transfiguration |
| The Finding in the Temple | The Institution of the Eucharist |
| **The Sorrowful Mysteries** | **The Glorious Mysteries** |
| The Agony in the Garden | The Resurrection |
| The Scourging at the Pillar | The Ascension |
| The Crowning with Thorns | The Descent of the Holy Spirit |
| The Carrying of the Cross | The Assumption of Mary |
| The Crucifixion and Death | The Coronation of Mary in Heaven |

# How to Pray the Rosary

1. Pray the Sign of the Cross and say the Apostles' Creed.
2. Pray the Lord's Prayer.
3. Pray three Hail Marys.
4. Pray the Glory to the Father.
5. Say the first mystery; then pray the Lord's Prayer.
6. Pray ten Hail Marys while meditating on the mystery.
7. Pray the Glory to the Father.
8. Say the second mystery; then pray the Lord's Prayer. Repeat 6 and 7 and continue with the third, fourth, and fifth mysteries in the same manner.
9. Pray the Hail, Holy Queen.

# Hail, Holy Queen

Hail, holy Queen, Mother of mercy,
hail, our life, our sweetness, and our hope.
To you we cry, the children of Eve;
to you we send up our sighs,
mourning and weeping in this land of exile.
Turn, then, most gracious advocate,
your eyes of mercy toward us;
lead us home at last
and show us the blessed fruit of your womb,
    Jesus:
O clement, O loving, O sweet Virgin Mary.

*Salve, Regina*

## Faith Fact

As the Mother of Jesus, the Son of God, Mary is called the Mother of God, the Queen of all Saints, and the Mother of the Church. There are many prayers and practices of devotion to Mary. One of the most popular is the Rosary. It focuses on the twenty mysteries that describe events in the lives of Jesus and Mary.

# Angelus

**V.** The angel spoke God's message to Mary,
**R.** and she conceived of the Holy
    Spirit.
Hail, Mary . . .

**V.** "I am the lowly servant of the Lord:
**R.** let it be done to me according to your word."
Hail, Mary . . .

**V.** And the Word became flesh,
**R.** and lived among us.
Hail, Mary . . .

**V.** Pray for us, holy Mother of God,
**R.** that we may become worthy of the
    promises of Christ.

Let us pray.

Lord,
fill our hearts with your grace:
once, through the message of an angel
you revealed to us the incarnation of
    your Son;
now, through his suffering and death
lead us to the glory of his resurrection.

We ask this through Christ our Lord.
Amen.

## Act of Faith

O God, we firmly believe that you are one God in three divine Persons, Father, Son, and Holy Spirit; we believe that your divine Son became man and died for our sins, and that he will come to judge the living and the dead. We believe these and all the truths that the holy Catholic Church teaches because you have revealed them, and you can neither deceive nor be deceived.

## Act of Hope

O God, relying on your almighty power and your endless mercy and promises, we hope to gain pardon for our sins, the help of your grace, and life everlasting, through the saving actions of Jesus Christ, our Lord and Redeemer.

## Act of Love

O God, we love you above all things, with our whole heart and soul, because you are all good and worthy of all love. We love our neighbor as ourselves for the love of you. We forgive all who have injured us and ask pardon of all whom we have injured.

# Holy, Holy, Holy Lord

**In English**

Holy, Holy, Holy Lord God of hosts.
Heaven and earth are full of your glory.
Hosanna in the highest.
Blessed is he who comes in the name of the Lord.
Hosanna in the highest.

**In Latin**

*Sanctus, Sanctus, Sanctus*
*Dominus Deus Sabaoth.*
*Pleni sunt coeli et terra gloria tua.*
   *Hosanna in excelsis.*

*Benedictus qui venit in nomine Domini.*
   *Hosanna in excelsis.*

# Agnus Dei (Lamb of God)

**In English**

Lamb of God, you take away the
  sins of the world,
   have mercy on us.
Lamb of God, you take away the
  sins of the world,
   have mercy on us.
Lamb of God, you take away the
  sins of the world,
   grant us peace.

**In Latin**

*Agnus Dei, qui tollis peccata mundi:*
*miserere nobis.*
*Agnus Dei, qui tollis peccata mundi:*
*miserere nobis.*
*Agnus Dei, qui tollis peccata mundi:*
*dona nobis pacem*

## Faith Fact

As members of the Catholic Church, we usually pray in the language that we speak, but we sometimes pray in Latin, the common language of the Church. The following are a couple of the common prayers of the Church in both English and Latin.

# WORDS OF FAITH

## A

**absolution** Words spoken by the priest during the Sacrament of Reconciliation. (245)

**authority** The power and the responsibility to lead others. (170)

## B

**Beatitudes** Teachings of Jesus that show the way to true happiness and tell the way to live in God's kingdom now and always. (117)

**blasphemy** The sin of showing contempt for the name of God, Jesus Christ, Mary, or the saints in words or action. (137)

## C

**canonized** Officially proclaimed a saint by the Church. Canonized saints have special feast days or memorials in the Church's calendar. (160)

**capital punishment** Taking the life of a person as punishment for a serious crime, such as murder. It is also called the death penalty. (198)

**charity** The virtue of love. It directs people to love God above all things and their neighbor as themselves, for the love of God. (127)

**community** A group of people who hold certain beliefs, hopes, and goals in common. (89)

**conscience** The gift from God that helps us know the difference between right and wrong and helps us choose what is right. (101)

**conversion** The process of turning our lives away from sin and toward the love of God and others. (243)

**Corporal Works of Mercy** Actions that meet the physical needs of others. (127)

**covenant** Sacred promise or agreement between God and humans. (55)

## D

**dignity** Is self-worth. Every human is worthy of respect because he or she is made in the image of God. (79)

**diversity** means variety, especially among people. (271)

## E

**envy** To resent or be sad from wanting for yourself what belongs to others. (261)

**Eucharist** The Sacrament through which Catholics are united with the life, death, and Resurrection of Jesus. (235)

## F

**faithful** To be steadfast and loyal in your commitment to God, just as he is faithful to you. (55)

**false witness** A misrepresentation of the truth. (208)

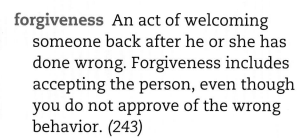

**forgiveness** An act of welcoming someone back after he or she has done wrong. Forgiveness includes accepting the person, even though you do not approve of the wrong behavior. (243)

**free will** The God-given ability to choose between good and evil. (99)

**gifts of the Holy Spirit** Seven powerful gifts we receive in Baptism and Confirmation. These gifts help us grow in our relationship with God and others. (278–279)

**grace** The gift of God's life in you. (99)

**Great Commandment** The two-fold command to love God above all and your neighbor as yourself. (125)

**greed** The desire to acquire earthly goods without limits or beyond one's needs. (261)

**heaven** The state of eternal happiness with God. (279)

**holiness** Being what God created you to be. You become holy, or Godlike, by sharing God's life of grace. (160)

**idolatry** The sin of worshiping an object or a person instead of God. It is letting anything or anyone become more important than God. (135)

**Immaculate Conception** The title for Mary that recognizes that God preserved her from sin from the first moment of her life. (163)

**justice** The virtue of giving to God and people what is due them. (271)

**kingdom of God** God's rule of peace, justice, and love that is here now, but has not yet come in its fullness. (151)

**laity** Name for all of the baptized people in the Church who share in God's mission but are not priests or consecrated sisters and brothers. (153)

**last judgment** The judgment that will occur at the end of time when Jesus returns to judge all who have ever lived. Then, all will fully see and understand God's plan for creation. (281)

**liturgical year** The cycle of feasts and seasons that makes up the Church's year of worship. (223)

**magisterium** The Church's teaching authority to interpret the word of God found in Scripture and Tradition. (173)

**martyr** A person who gives up his or her life to witness to the truth of the faith. (207)

**321**

**mission** To be sent to share the good news of Jesus and the kingdom of God. *(271)*

**modesty** The virtue that helps people dress, talk, and act in appropriate ways. *(189)*

**morality** Living in right relationship with God, yourself and others. It is putting your beliefs into action. *(91)*

**mortal sin** A serious sin that destroys your relationship with God. *(80)*

**murder** The deliberate killing of an innocent person. *(199)*

**obey** To do things or act in certain ways that are requested by those in authority. *(189)*

**Original Sin** The choice of the first humans to disobey God. *(53)*

**parish** A Catholic community with shared spiritual beliefs and worship. *(91)*

**particular judgment** The individual judgment by God at the time of your death. *(281)*

**Paschal mystery** The mystery of Jesus' suffering, death, Resurrection, and Ascension. *(223)*

**patron saint** A model of faith and protector for you. *(163)*

**penance** The name for the prayer, offering, or good work the priest gives you in the Sacrament of Reconciliation. *(245)*

**perjury** A lie that is told in a court of law. *(208)*

**precepts of the Church** Some of the minimum requirements given by Church leaders for deepening your relationship with God and the Church. *(173)*

**providence** God's loving care for all things; God's will and plan for creation. *(45)*

**reparation** The action taken to repair the damage done through a sin. *(209)*

**revelation** The way God tells humans about himself and makes his plan known. *(45)*

**Sacrament of the Anointing of the Sick** Brings Jesus' healing touch to strengthen, comfort, and forgive the sins of those who are seriously ill or close to death. *(245)*

**Sacrament of Reconciliation** The Sacrament that celebrates God's mercy and forgiveness and a sinner's reconciliation with God and the Church through the absolution of the priest. *(243)*

**Sacraments** Signs that give grace. Sacraments were instituted by Christ and are celebrated by his Church. *(233)*

**saint** A person whom the Church declares has led a holy life and is enjoying eternal life with God in heaven. *(161)*

**Scripture** Another name for the Bible. Scripture is the word of God written in human words. *(45)*

**sin** The deliberate thought, word, deed, or omission contrary to the law of God. *(81)*

**social sin** A sinful social structure or institution that builds up over time so that it affects the whole society. *(81)*

**soul** The spiritual part of a human that lives forever. *(79)*

**stewardship** The human responsibility to care for God's creation and to respect all life as a gift from God. *(261)*

**suicide** The taking of one's own life. *(198)*

**Ten Commandments** The summary of laws that God gave to Moses on Mount Sinai. They tell us what is necessary in order to love God and others. *(64)*

**Triduum** The celebration of the passion, death and Resurrection of Christ. The Triduum begins on Holy Thursday evening and concludes on Easter Sunday night. *(225)*

**venial sin** A less serious sin that weakens your relationship with God. *(80)*

**vocation** God's call to love and serve him and others. *(151)*

**vows** Solemn promises that are made to or before God. *(189)*

**worship** To adore and praise God especially in prayer and in liturgy. *(135)*

Note: Boldfaced numbers refer to pages on which the terms are defined.

### Illustration Credits

8–9 Frank Ordaz; 12–13 Maurie Manning; 16–17 Simone Boni; 20–21 Dan Brown; 28–29 Joel Spector; 32 Nick Harris; 36 Dennis Lyall. 42 (bkgd) Stacey Schuett; 44 (bl) James M. Effler; 45 (br) Judy Stead; 50 (bl) Lois Woolley; 52 (b) Dan Brown; 54 (bl) Michael Jaroszko; 55 (tr) Michael Jaroszko; 55 (br) Judy Stead; 60 (bl) Lois Woolley; 61 (b) Ezra Tucker; 62 (bl) Tom Newsom; 63 (cr) Mark Stevens; 64 (bl) Corey Wolfe; 65 (br) Judy Stead; 67 (bl) Judy Stead; 67 (br) Judy Stead; 67 (tl) Judy Stead; 67 (tr) Judy Stead; 70 (bl) Lois Woolley; 73 (cr) Judy Stead. 81 (br) Judy Stead; 86 (bl) Lois Woolley; 88 (bl) Cathy Diefendorf; 96 (bl) Lois Woolley; 98 (l) Jeff Preston; 98 (br) Jeff Preston; 100 (bl) Jeff Spackman; 106 (bl) Lois Woolley. 114 (b) Peter Church; 116 (br) Steve Adler; 122 (cr) Judy Stead; 122 (bl) Lois Woolley; 124 (bl) Roger Payne; 126 (bl) Karen Patkau; 131 (b) Judy Stead; 132 (bl) Lois Woolley; 134 (b) Adam Hook; 137 (br) Judy Stead; 142 (bl) Lois Woolley. 148 (tl) Yvonne Gilbert; 149 (br) Yvonne Gilbert; 150 (b) Mike Jaroszko; 151 (bl) Judy Stead; 158 (bl) Lois Woolley; 160 (bl) Philip Howe; 161 (cr) Philip Howe; 164 (cl) Lois Woolley; 164 (cr) Lois Woolley; 164 (tl) Lois Woolley; 164 (tr) Lois Woolley; 168 (cr) Judy Stead; 168 (bl) Lois Woolley; 170 (b) Dominick D'Andrea; 171 (cr) Dominick D'Andrea; 178 (bl) Lois Woolley. 187 (tr) Philip Howe; 194 (bl) Lois Woolley; 197 (tr) Robert Sauber; 204 (bl) Lois Woolley; 206 (b) Jeff Preston; 214 (bl) Lois Woolley. 220 (cl) Philip Howe; 230 (bl) Lois Woolley; 231 (br) Philip Howe; 232 (b) Jeff Preston; 234 (b) Yuan Lee; 240 (bl) Lois Woolley; 242 (b) Doug Fryer; 245 (br) Adam Hook; 250 (bl) Lois Woolley. 258 (bl) Peter Church; 261 (cr) Kevin Torline; 266 (bl) Lois Woolley; 270 (b) Dean Kennedy; 276 (bl) Lois Woolley; 278 (bkgd) Kevin Torline; 283 (cr) Judy Stead; 286 (bl) Lois Woolley.

### Photo Credits

iii Gabe Palmer/Corbis; 1 l Rubberball Productions; 1 r Comstock Images; 2 Richard Hutchings/PhotoEdit; 6-7 bg Photomondo/Getty Images; 7 inset Father Gene Plaisted, OSC; 10-11 bg PhotoAlto/Creatas; 10-11 fg Richard Hutchings; 11 c Richard Hutchings; 14-15 bg Don Farrall/Photodisc/Getty Images; 15 inset Ariel Skelley/Corbis; 18-19 Benelux Press/Index Stock/Photolibrary; 22-23 bg Fridmar Damm/Corbis; 23 c Richard Hutchings; 23 b Richard Hutchings; 24-25 Richard Hurtchings/PhotoEdit; 26-27 bg Jakob Helbig/cultura/Corbis; 27 inset C Squared Studios/Photodisc/Getty Images; 30-31 t Corel; 30-31 b Daryl Benson/Masterfile; 31 fg Richard Hutchings; 34-35 bg Rich Reid/Getty Images; 35 inset Tetra Images/Corbis; 38-39 bg Corel; 39 t Photodisc/Getty Images; 39 b Richard Hutchings; 40 l Eric Camden; 40 l Bob Davidson Photography/Getty Images; 40 c Brian Minnich; 41 fg Eric Camden; 41 bg Bob Davidson Photography/Getty Images45 Thinkstock/Comstock/Getty Images; 46 t Eric Camden; 46 b Eric Camden; 48 Ed McDonald; 51 Brian Minnich; 52 cl Jacqui Hurst; 53 t Katie S. Atkinson/Getty Images; 53 b Sonny Senser; 56 b Eric Camden; 58 Bill Wittman; 63 Sonny Senser; 65 John Nakata/Corbis; 66 cr Marcelo Santos/The Image Bank/Getty Images; 66 bl Eric Camden; 66 br Mary Kate Denny/Stone/Getty Images; 68 The Mazer Corporation; 70 Ed McDonald; 71 tl Kurt Stier/Corbis; 71 bl Ivo Von Renner/Stone/Getty Images; 71 bc D. Falconer/PhotoLink/Getty Images; 71 br David Young-Wolffe/PhotoEdit; 72 t David Young-Wolffe/PhotoEdit; 72 c Jose Luis Pelaez, Inc./Corbis; 72-73 b Terrance Klassen/Ponka Wonka; 73 inset Sonny Senser; 76 l Eric Camden; 76 l John Connell/Corbis; 76 c Ed McDonald; 76 r Royalty-Free/Getty Images; 76 r Amos Morgan/Photodisc/Getty Images; 76 r Fuse/Getty Images; 76 r Corbis/Fotosearch; 77 bg John Connell/Corbis; 77 fg Eric Camden; 78 Bettman/Corbis; 79 c Ariel Skelley/Corbis; 79 b Jim Whitmer; 80 LWA-Dann Tardif; 81 James W. Porter/Corbis; 82 t Bill Wittman/Ponka Wonka; 82 b Sonny Senser; 84 Paul Vozdic/Stone/Getty Images; 86 Jack Holtel/Photographik Company; 87 Ed McDonald; 89 c Cleve Bryant/PhotoEdit; 89 b Jim Whitmer; 90 Portland Art Museum/Gift of the Samuel H. Kress Foundation; 91 Richard Hutchings/Photo Edit; 92 Arthur Tilley/Taxi/Getty Images; 94 Tom & Dee Ann McCarthy/Corbis; 97 bg Royalty-Free/Getty Images; 97 t Amos Morgan/Photodisc/Getty Images; 97 c Fuse/Getty Images; 97 b Corbis/Fotosearch; 99 t Houghton Mifflin Harcourt; 99 b David Young-Wolffe/PhotoEdit; 101 Sonny Senser; 102 t Amos Morgan/Photodisc/Getty Images; 102 c Ed McDonald; 102 b Royalty-Free/Corbis; 104 Jeff Grenberg/PhotoEdit; 106 Brian Leng/Corbis; 107 bg Digital Vision/Getty Images; 107 c Our Sunday Visitor Curriculum Division; 107 bl St. George Church; 107 br St. George Church; 108-109 bg Digital Vision/Getty Images; 108 inset St. George Church; 112 l Ed McDonald; 112 c Brian Minnich; 112 r Ed McDonald; 112-113 bg Ed McDonald; 115 Sonny Senser; 117 Ed McDonald; 118 Bill Wittman; 120 Diane Macdonald/Stockbyte/Getty Images; 123 c Brian Minnich; 123 bl Ed McDonald; 123 br Brian Minnich; 125 l Kwame Zikomo/SuperStock; 125 r Steve Skjold/Alamy; 127 Andrew Bret Wallis/Getty Images; 128 c Myrleen Ferguson Cate/PhotoEdit; 128 bl Michael Newman/PhotoEdit; 128 br Eric Camden; 130 Father Gene Plaisted, OSC; 133 Ed McDonald; 135 c Bill Wittman; 135 b Jim Whitmer; 136 Myrleen Ferguson Cate/PhotoEdit; 137 Paul Barton/Corbis; 138 Eric Camden; 140 Eric Camden; 142 Ed McDonald; 143 c Mobile Loaves & Fishes; 143 bl Steve Skjold/Alamy; 143 bc Joseph Harnish; 143 br Joseph Harnish; 144 c Mobile Loaves & Fishes; 144 b Mobile Loaves & Fishes; 145 c Sonny Senser; 145 bl Myrleen Ferguson Cate/PhotoEdit; 145 bcl Joseph Harnish; 145 bcr Myrleen Ferguson Cate/PhotoEdit; 145 br Joseph Harnish; 148 c Culver Pictures, Inc./SuperStock ; 148 cl Culver Pictures, Inc./SuperStock ; 148 cr David Turnley/Corbis; 148 r Eric Camden; 151 Philippe Lissac/Godong/Corbis; 152 Father Gene Plaisted, OSC; 153 Muscular Dystrophy Association; 154 Father Gene Plaisted, OSC; 156 Eric Camden; 158 Jack Holtel/Photographik Company; 159 t Culver Pictures, Inc./SuperStock; 159 c Culver Pictures, Inc./SuperStock; 159 b David Turnley/Corbis; 162 Arte & Immagini srl/CORBIS; 163 Father Gene Plaisted, OSC; 166 t Father Gene Plaisted, OSC; 166 cl Father Gene Plaisted, OSC; 166 cr Father Gene Plaisted, OSC; 166 bl Father Gene Plaisted, OSC; 166 br Father Gene Plaisted, OSC; 169 Eric Camden; 171 Jim Whitmer; 172 KAI PFAFFENBACH/Reuters/Corbis; 173 Father Gene Plaisted, OSC; 174 t Digital Vision/Getty Images; 174 b Sonny Senser; 176 SuperStock/SuperStock ; 178 Brooklyn Productions/The Image Bank/Getty Images; 179 bg Jack Hollingsworth/Photodisc/Getty Images; 179 bl Michael Newman/PhotoEdit; 179 bc Norbert von der Groeben/The Image Works; 179 br Vince Streano/Corbis; 180-181 bg Jack Hollingsworth/Photodisc/Getty Images ; 180 t Saint Charles Borromeo Catholic School; 180 c Saint Charles Borromeo Catholic School; 180 bl Saint Charles Borromeo Catholic School; 180 br Saint Charles Borromeo Catholic School; 181 br Sonny Senser; 184 l Patrick Johns/Corbis; 184 l Ariel Skelley/Corbis; 184 c Eric Camden; 184 r Eric Camden; 184-185 bg Patrick Johns/Corbis; 185 b Ariel Skelley/Corbis; 186 Eric Camden; 187 Jim Whitmer; 188 Ken Reid; 189 Joel Sartore/National Geographic/Getty Images; 190 Peter Mason/Image Bank/Getty Images; 192 Frank Siteman/PhotoEdit; 194 Roy Morsch/Corbis; 195 Ed McDonald; 196 t Bettman/Corbis; 196 c David Turnley/Corbis; 196 bl Pierre Perrin/Zoko/Sygma/Corbis; 196-197 br Bettman/Corbis; 197 c Royalty-Free/Getty Images; 198 Stephen Simpson/Taxi/Getty Images; 199 Jim Whitmer; 200 bl David Young-Wolffe/PhotoEdit; 200 br SW Productions/Photodisc/Getty Images; 202 Andy Sacks/Stone/Getty Images; 205 Eric Camden; 207 l Bettman/Corbis; 207 r Bettman/Corbis; 208 Jose Luis Pelaez, Inc./Corbis; 209 Tony Freeman/PhotoEdit; 210 Sonny Senser; 212 Photodisc/Getty Images; 214 Ariel Skelley/Corbis; 215 c Mark Bradshaw; 215 bl Mark Bradshaw; 215 br Mark Anderson/Rubberball/Alamy; 216-217 bg Mark Anderson/Rubberball/Alamy; 216 c Mark Bradshaw; 216 bl Mark Bradshaw; 220 l Frank Cezus/Taxi/Getty Images; 220 l Frank Cezus/Taxi/Getty Images; 220 l Frank Cezus/Taxi/Getty Images; 220 l Frank Cezus/Taxi/Getty Images; 220 l Eric Camden; 220 r Ed McDonald; 220-221 bg Keith Wood/Corbis; 221 tcl Frank Cezus/Taxi/Getty Images; 221 cl Frank Cezus/Taxi/Getty Images; 171 bl Eric Camden; 171 bcl Frank Cezus/Taxi/Getty Images; 171 br Frank Cezus/Taxi/Getty Images; 222 t Michael Keller; 222 c Tobi Corney/Stone/Getty Images; 222 bl Pascal Crapet/Stone/Getty Images; 222 br Sonny Senser; 225 Father Gene Plaisted, OSC; 226 tl Myrleen Ferguson Cate/PhotoEdit; 226 tr Bill Wittman; 226 cl Lane Oatey/Getty Images; 226 cr SW Productions/Photodisc/Getty Images; 226 b Jim Whitmer; 228 Eric Camden; 230 Sonny Senser; 233 cl Elio Ciol/Corbis; 233 c Ed McDonald; 233 cr Royalty-Free/Corbis; 233 bl Jim Whitmer; 233 bcr Royalty-Free/Corbis; 235 Myrleen Ferguson Cate/PhotoEdit; 236 Bill Wittman; 238 Bill Wittman; 240 Ed McDonald; 241 Ed McDonald; 243 Jim Whitmer; 244 Father Gene Plaisted, OSC; 246 Eric Camden; 248 Tony Freeman/PhotoEdit; 251 b Bob Daemmrich/PhotoEdit; 252 t A. Ramey/PhotoEdit; 252 b Billy Hustace/Stone/Getty Images; 253 David Young-Wolffe/PhotoEdit; 256 l Brian Minnich; 256 c Brian Minnich; 256 r Ed McDonald; 256-257 bg Brian Minnich; 259 t George Disario/Corbis; 259 b Jim Whitmer; 260 Victoria Bowen; 262 Sonny Senser; 264 David Young-Wolffe/PhotoEdit; 267 Brian Minnich; 268-269 bg Maryknoll Minstries; 268 c Maryknoll Bolivia Photos; 268 b Maryknoll Minstries; 269 t Maryknoll Minstries; 269 c Maryknoll Minstries; 269 b Jim Whitmer; 271 Jim Whitmer; 272 Eric Camden; 274 Sonny Senser; 276 Joe Carlson/Corbis; 277 bg Ed McDonald; 277 fg Ed McDonald; 279 Jim Whitmer; 280 t Michael Newman/PhotoEdit; 280 b Peter Frank/Corbis; 281 l Larry Mulvehill/Corbis; 281 r Guy Cali/Corbis; 282 moodboard/Getty Images; 284 Peter Burian/Corbis; 287 l Mario Tama/Getty Images; 287 r Robert Brenner/PhotoEdit; 288 c Jeff Grenberg/PhotoEdit; 288 bl Dennis MacDonald/PhotoEdit; 288 br Lon C Dieh/PhotoEdit; 289 b Dennis MacDonald/PhotoEdit; 293 t Myrleen Ferguson Cate/PhotoEdit; 292-293 b Richard Hutchings; 294 Ingram Publishing; 295 Richard Hutchings; 296 Father Gene Plaisted, OSC; 298 t Osservatore Romano/POOL/Reuters/Corbis; 298 b Jupiter Images/Getty Images; 300 l Father Gene Plaisted, OSC; 300 r Photos.com; 301 l Corel; 301 r Corel; 305 rubberball/Getty Images; 306 t C Squared Studios/Photodisc/Getty Images; 306 c Photodisc/Getty Images; 306 bl Photodisc/Getty Images; 306 br Photodisc/Getty Images; 309 Thinkstock/Getty Images; 310-311 Thinkstock/Getty Images; 312-313 Thinkstock/Getty Images; 314-315 Thinkstock/Getty Images; 316-317 Thinkstock/Getty Images; 318-319 Thinkstock/Getty Images

### Acknowledgments

For permission to reprint copyrighted material, grateful acknowledgment is made to the following sources:

*Liturgy Training Publications, 1800 North Hermitage Avenue, Chicago, IL 60622, 1-800-933-1800, www.ltp.org:* From "Prayer for Our Lady of Guadalupe" (Retitled: "Prayer for Our Lady of Guadalupe Day") in *Blessings and Prayers through the Year: A Resource for School and Parish* by Elizabeth McMahon Jeep. Text © 2004 by Archdiocese of Chicago.

*Jack Prelutsky:* From "Me I Am!" in *The Random House Book of Poetry* by Jack Prelutsky. Text copyright by Jack Prelutsky.

*Patricia Joyce Shelly:* Lyrics from "All Grownups, All Children" by Patricia Joyce Shelly. Lyrics © 1977 by Patricia Joyce Shelly.

*Twenty-Third Publications, A Division of Bayard:* "Grail Prayer" from *500 Prayers for Catholic Schools & Parish Youth Groups* by Filomena Tassi and Peter Tassi. Text copyright © 2004 by Filomena Tassi and Peter Tassi.

*United States Conference of Catholic Bishops, Inc., Washington, D.C.:* English translation of "Hail, Holy Queen" (*Salve, Regina*) from *Catholic Household Blessings and Prayers*. Translation copyright © 1989 by United States Catholic Conference, Inc.

*Viking Penguin, a division of Penguin Group (USA) Inc.:* "The Creation" from *God's Trombones* by James Weldon Johnson. Text copyright 1927 by The Viking Press, Inc.; text copyright renewed © 1955 by Grace Nail Johnson.